The KINGDOM Of GOD Is SPIRITUAL WARFARE

You cannot escape this battle, but you can triumph through faith in CHRIST JESUS.

David Kwadwo Okai, PhD.

Copyright © 2014 by David Kwadwo Okai, PhD.

The Kingdom Of God Is Spiritual Warfare
You cannot escape this battle, but you can triumph through
faith in CHRIST JESUS.
by David Kwadwo Okai, PhD.

Printed in the United States of America

ISBN 9781629527246

All rights reserved solely by the author. The author guarantees all contents are original and do not infringe upon the legal rights of any other person or work. No part of this book may be reproduced in any form without the permission of the author. The views expressed in this book are not necessarily those of the publisher.

Unless otherwise indicated, Bible quotations are taken from the King James Version, (Hebrew-Greek Key Word Study Bible). Copyright © 1991 unless stated otherwise.

www.xulonpress.com

"The Kingdom of GOD is Spiritual Warfare: You cannot Escape this Battle, but You can Triumph through Faith in CHRIST JESUS"

ACKNOWLEDGMENTS

*I*t takes the prudence, superintendence, and power of my three Member consultant team of the Father, the Son Jesus Christ, and the Holy Spirit to complete this biblical theology of "The Kingdom of GOD is spiritual warfare: You cannot escape this battle, but you can triumph through faith in CHRIST JESUS." To God be the glory, Amen.

I acknowledge my wife Dinah for standing with me for the past 35 years in marriage, and 22 years in ministry (in Ghana and the USA). Your love accelerates the triumph of JESUS CHRIST in our daily combat with satanic forces. I sincerely love you and recognize you as a Godsend gift to me.

My children (Pastor Daniel, Ernest, Angela, Kingsley, and Michael) fervently support me in my life and ministry. You are pleasant fragrance in the annals of the Okais and the Kingdom of God.

My maternal grandmother (Eno Akua Nsiah), my siblings (Kwasi Prempeh, Yaw Akrasi Sarpong, and Charles Akrasi Boateng), and their respective families; you are part of my life and ministry.

My late parents (Mr. Joe Okai and Madam Akua Agyeiwaa), my late in-laws (Opanin Kwasi Boamah and Madam Abena Agyeiwaa), my late siblings (Kwame Attakora, Charity Aduako, and Lt. Col. Richard Amponsem Boateng – Commander of 4th Battalion of Infantry-Kumasi); your memories are fresh in my life and ministry.

All my teachers, instructors, professors, and administrators from Kindergarten, Elementary and High Schools, Mid Ghana Bible College Kumasi, Ashland Theological Seminary USA, Southwest Bible College and Seminary USA, Assemblies of God Theological Seminary USA, and Louisiana Baptist University USA. Thanks for the impact you have had in my life and ministry.

The Assemblies of God Ghana and the United States of America, my ministry partners and sponsors, (pastors, churches, and individual families), Charity Assembly of God Juaben Ashanti Ghana, Gospel Radiant Assembly of God Praaso A/A Ghana, Church of the King-Berkley, Brightmoor Christian Church-Novi, and Resurrection & Life Church-Berkley Michigan USA. I appreciate your excellent partnership.

My pastors (Rev. Mathew K. Opoku and late Rev. Paul Kwame Yeboah); thanks for helping me to identify God's calling upon my life.

The Bradshaws, the Kjos, the Pops, the Muhlings, the Leachs, the Cholettes, the Sullivans, the Frechettes, the Buchans, the Blaggs, the Elartons, the Murrays, the Williams, the Galindos, the Tanners, the Pages, the Fosters, the Rowmanoskis, the Haleys, the Krists, the Hlavins, the Nagles, the Tanners, the Kues, the Dalabas, the Warrens, the Diehls, the Trasks, the Mattiuzzos, the Krages, the Aikins, the Kennedys, the Garcias the Shumakes, the Samoneks, the Bukharts, the Thomas, the Fonsekas, Michelle Rincon and the Boonzelaars, Vespas, Takyis, and Dorseys; your immense support cannot be overlooked.

Students I have taught at Ashland Seminary (Detroit center, New Beginnings Cathedral, and Greater Emmanuel Church of God in Christ), and Northpoint Bible College (Grand Rapids campus); thanks for your thought provoking questions in class.

A friend of mine says, "Good friends are God's...let's cherish and appreciate them." My friends from age 5 to now; your diverse contributions cannot be underestimated. I appreciate you.

SPECIAL DEDICATION

I DEDICATE THIS BOOK TO
MY SWEET HEART DINAH OKAI

ENDORSEMENTS

"David has put together a thorough examination of the Kingdom of God and the ongoing spiritual battle that rages around us in these last days."

David Keeny, ThD
Dean of Biblical Studies
Louisiana Baptist University, Shreveport

"With a thorough, systematic, and refreshing scholastic approach, Dr. Okai has theorized and clearly demonstrated the correlation between the kingdom of God and spiritual warfare – two of the most misunderstood and abused subjects in Christian orthodoxy today. For those of us who crave daily to consistent victorious living in Christ Jesus, facilitated by the power and enablement of the Holy Spirit, this book is a welcome source of profound spiritual nourishment for our faith… A must read for all Christian denominations, Bible students, pastors, and teachers in seminary and the church."

Rev. Kwame Owusu-Baafi
Senior Pastor, International Baptist Church of Dakar, Senegal

"Whether we want to admit it or not we are at war. The Bible tells us that we struggle not against flesh and blood, but against an enemy who is invisible. David Okai has done an excellent job of creating awareness of the ongoing warfare that we battle every day. But we as Christians are protected, and we have hope."

Sandra Cory, D.R.E.
Executive Vice President of Administration
Louisiana Baptist University, Shreveport

"David Okai has produced a masterful treatise on the kingdom of God as it relates to spiritual warfare and the mission of the church in the world. Even though he speaks from his current location as an American scholar, his African heritage clearly colors how he approaches the subject. In fact, Dr. Okai writes about the kingdom of God as one who has experienced it in his own life! Those who long to encounter the voice of the global church will recognize the authenticity and great value of this book. Virtually, every aspect of the subject is explored and explicated. Few have operationalize "kingdom of God" as well as Dr. Okai. In truth, this book so effectively weaves together biblical theology and practical theology that it could serve as a handbook for those seeking to do kingdom based ministry."

William Payne, PhD
The Harlan and Wilma Hollewell
Professor of Evangelism and Missions
Ashland Theological Seminary, Ashland
Author: "American Methodism: Past and Future Growth"

"The Kingdom of God is spiritual warfare" is a brilliant, down-to-earth look at the theology of the Kingdom of God and its implications of spiritual warfare in daily lives. In this book David Okai goes to great length tracing the meaning and the nature of the Kingdom of God from the Old Testament through the New Testament, and relates them with spiritual warfare. Dr. Okai does not only write passionately about the Kingdom theology, but pin-points relevant biblical and theological truths to support his thesis that "the Kingdom of God is spiritual warfare, you cannot escape it, but you can triumph through faith in Christ Jesus." Both Christians and non-Christians

ENDORSEMENTS

will find this book extremely helpful in understanding the dynamics of the Kingdom of God and how they interface with daily life, I endorse it as a must-read for all and sundry."

Rev. Dr. Paul Frimpong-Manso
General Superintendent
Assemblies of God, Ghana

"Dr. David Okai's book about the Kingdom of God is based on scripture and presents a clear and concise explanation of the way that our lives are affected by the ongoing battle. Dr. Okai lists and discusses the issues that we encounter in our daily lives which are the results of spiritual warfare and offers a way to deal with such issues. I highly recommend this book as a resource for teachers, students, and for all people in ministry."

Sharon Marshall, DMin, LPC
Professor of Counseling
Ashland Theological Seminary, Detroit Center

"David Okai is a man who knows spiritual warfare. I had the privilege to travel with David to his hometown and walked in the streets David walked as a pagan, an alcoholic, and a lost soul. God searched for David and saved him so dramatically, delivering him from addiction. At that moment, David entered God's Kingdom with all his heart. David's thirst for hunger and righteousness has filled him up. This book is as a result of David's learning and his life. David Okai writes from what he knows, both with his head and his heart. As you read this book of the Kingdom of God you will see the battle that rages and understand your part in advancing gospel against the gates of Hell. Well done Dr. Okai, well done. This book is a result of a faithful son, soldier, and servant of God. The Kingdom of God is advancing and you are a part of this spiritual warfare—this book will help you discover if you are fighting with God or against God."

Rev. Steve Bradshaw
(Former Director of Church Planting and Missions,
Assemblies of God Michigan District)
Lead Pastor
Lift Church, Venice, Florida

"This treatise on "the Kingdom of God is spiritual warfare" is theologically sound, cross-culturally applicable, and practically relevantly. In fact, spiritual warfare is real as succinctly unveiled by Dr. Okai in his book. I do recommend for all those who are involved in Kingdom based ministry as a handy manual on spiritual warfare."

Rev. Dr. Tito Adjei
Regional Superintendent
Assemblies of God, Ashanti Region
Senior Pastor
Grace Assembly of God, Bronkrong–Kumasi

TABLE OF CONTENTS

PREFACE xv

1. WHAT IS "THE KINGDOM OF GOD?" 19
   A. The Meaning of "the Kingdom of God" 19
   B. The King of "the Kingdom of God" 21
   C. The Message of "the Kingdom of God" 22
   D. The Partakers of "the Kingdom of God" 22
   E. The Condition to Partake in "the Kingdom of God" 23

2. THE NATURE OF "THE KINGDOM OF GOD" 25
   A. "The Kingdom of God" is God's Rule and Reign 25
   B. "The Kingdom of God" is Soteriological 26
   C. The Mystery of "the Kingdom of God" 27
   D. The Imminence of "the Kingdom of God" 27
   E. "The Kingdom of God" is Eschatological 29
   F. "The Kingdom of God" is Dynamic 30

3. THE NATURE OF SPIRITUAL WARFARE 33
   A. The Meaning of Spiritual Warfare 33
   B. The Parties Involved in Spiritual Warfare 34
   C. The Origin of Spiritual Warfare 43
   D. The Battlefield of Spiritual Warfare 44
   E. The Weapons of Spiritual Warfare 59
   F. Waging Spiritual Warfare 65

4. OLD TESTAMENT ANTECEDENT OF "THE KINGDOM OF GOD" IS SPIRITUAL WARFARE 86
   A. From Creation to the Tower of Babel 87
   B. The Patriarchs 94
   C. Israel and the Nations 105

5. "THE KINGDOM OF GOD" IS SPIRITUAL WARFARE IN THE NEW TESTAMENT 124
   A. John the Baptist 124
   B. Jesus Christ 126
   C. The Holy Spirit 138
   D. The First Century Believers in Jesus Christ 140

6. DIVERSE DOCTRINES AND PRAXIS OF "THE KINGDOM OF GOD" IS SPIRITUAL WARFARE. 149
   A. Weak and Weird Ecclesiological Doctrines and Praxis 149
   B. Doctrines and Praxis of World Religions 151
   C. Christocentric Doctrine and Praxis 153

7. THE CONSUMATION OF "THE KINGDOM OF GOD" IS SPIRITUAL WARFARE 156
   A. Pre-Second Advent of Jesus Christ 156
   B. Post-Second Advent of Jesus Christ 158

8. CONCLUSION 161
9. BIBLIOGRAPHY 167

PREFACE

The escalating rate of life struggles is very vivid in the eyes of all peoples in all nations. Every human being attributes this inescapable life battle to different sources. Developed countries, developing countries, underdeveloped countries, and third world countries alike have their crucial warfare. What is causing excruciating battles in individual lives, marriages, families, communities, schools (kindergarten, nursery, elementary, high schools, colleges, universities, seminaries), court system, parliament, white house, nations, etc? Ignorance of the source of your daily combat, and how to live a persistent victorious life triggers horrible torments, deep seated depression, outrageous hopelessness, and suicidal. In this book the Holy Spirit unfolds biblical and theological truth that "the Kingdom of God is spiritual warfare: You cannot escape this battle, but you triumph through faith in Jesus Christ." This undeniable truth facilitates you to appropriate the victory of Jesus Christ as a partaker of the Kingdom of God.

Do you believe the reality and existence of God as the Creator of the universe? Your conception about God and the Kingdom of God is an ongoing spiritual warfare in you as a human being created in the likeness of God. You struggle within yourself to either believe or disbelieve this truth. You wrestle to take initiatives to please either the God of the Kingdom or to appease your god. Regrettably, some church leaders (the clergy) in Catholicism, Protestantism, Pentecostalism, Charismatics, other denominations, as well as leaders of world religions are ignorant that they are unceasingly engaged in fierce battle in all spheres of their lives. With their "big and loud microphones" some church leaders promote whatever is "good" in their eyes, and in the eyes of wayward humanity just to win hollow support, ill-recognition, and doom-trapped prominence. Even some professors, instructors, lecturers, teachers, and counselors in Christian schools (eg., Seminaries, Christian Colleges, and Universities) are activists of detestable and indecent deeds.

Some, if not many political appointees (presidents, prime ministers, heads of state, senators, congressmen and women, ministers of state, parliamentarians, judges, ambassadors, and others) defiantly endorse, propagate, engage in abominable deeds like lesbianism, homosexuality, and similar indecent and immoral acts. Ignorant of demonic schemes and devices, such leaders cover Satan and his destructive works. Unfortunately, such leaders categorize these detestable acts under "equal rights", "freedom of choice", and other egocentric lusts.

Do you believe the existence of Satan and his demonic forces? The serpent, also known as Satan, Lucifer, the devil, arch enemy, the liar, the tempter, the slanderer, the accuser of the brethren, and the deceiver craftily pollutes the reasoning faculties of humanity to rebuff the faithfulness, integrity, and sovereignty of God (Gen 3:2-6). God forbid, I am neither exaggerating Satan, nor am I attempting to demonize humanity, the forest, the sea, the sky, mountains, valleys, etc. Rather, I am led by the Spirit of God to write a biblical theology of "the Kingdom of God is spiritual warfare: You cannot escape this battle, but you can triumph through faith in Jesus Christ."

Are you convincingly conscious that you are God's creation after God's image and likeness *(imago Dei)*? Are you still battling with the false doctrine that you did evolve from apes and monkeys? In the light of God and His Word, all human beings irrespective of color or gender are descendants of Adam and Eve (Gen. 2:19-24).

In this book, I strive with the prudence, audacity, discernment, and authority of God to pinpoint biblical and theological truth that the Kingdom of God is spiritual warfare. You agree with me that in every battle there is the winner and the looser. In this battle, Jesus Christ is the winner while Satan is the looser. The only clue to emerge a winner in this fierce battle that is waged by Satan and his agents is to align your faith in the One who is strong and mighty in all battles (Ps. 24: 7-10), the One who triumphed over Satan, sin, and death on your behalf (John 19:30; Acts 2:23-Col. 2:15), the One who paid the prize for your sin (Rom. 4:25), the One who imputes the righteousness of God upon your life through your faith in Him (II Cor. 5:21), the Lord of all lords and the King of all kings (Rev. 17:14)—Jesus Christ the Son of God.

I pray that the Holy Spirit illumines your reasoning faculties as you read and study this biblical and theological exposition of the inescapable warfare to enable you genuinely embrace the love of the Father, appropriate the triumph of His Son Jesus Christ in your life, and live a Spirit-filled, Spirit-consumed, Spirit empowered, and Spirit-led victorious life in spite of the escalating traumatic times in the world.

CHAPTER 1

WHAT IS "THE KINGDOM OF GOD"

The Meaning of "the Kingdom of God"

"The term "kingdom of God" or "kingdom of Heaven" signifies God's (see God) sovereign, dynamic and eschatological (see Eschatology) rule."[1] "The Kingdom of God" and "the Kingdom of the heavens" are linguistic variations of the same idea."[2] In his rich contribution to this subject Caragounis says:

The Gospels use three terms to express the idea of the kingdom of God: *he basileia tou theou* ("the kingdom of God"), *he basileia ton ouranon* ("the kingdom of (the) Heavens[s]") and the absolute *he basileia* ("the kingdom"). The equivalence of the first two expressions is indicated by the content, context and interchangeability in the Gospels.[3]

Furthermore, Caragounis states:
The Greek for "the kingdom of (the) Heaven(s) is a literal translation of the later Jewish *malkut samayim* (e.g., *2 Apoc. Bar. 73; 3 Apoc. Bar.* 11:2; *As. Mos.* 10; *Pss. Sol.* 17:4; 1QSb 3:5; *m. Ber.*

---

[1] Chrys C. Caragounis, "Kingdom of God/Kingdom of Heaven," in *Dictionary of Jesus and the Gospels:* ed. Joel B. Green (Downers Grove: InterVarsity Press, 1992), 417.

[2] George Eldon Ladd, "Kingdom of Christ, God, Heaven," in *Evangelical Dictionary of Theology:* ed. Walter A. Elwell (Grand Rapids: Baker Books, 1999), 607.

[3] Caragounis, "Kingdom of God/Kingdom of Heaven," 417.

2.2, 5; *y. Ber.* 4a; 7b), where "Heaven" replaces "God" out of reverence, as *donay* ("lord," "master") had replaced *Yahweh* ("Lord" and *makom* ("place") in due time replaced *samayim* ("Heaven") (Dalman, 91-101). The kingdom of God is also referred to by the absolute "kingdom" when the reference is obvious.[4] While Matthew preserves the Semitic idiom, the other Gospel writers render it into idiomatic Greek.[5] Therefore, I will use these two expressions "the kingdom of God" and "the kingdom of heaven[s]" interchangeably in this book.

Dr. Ridderbos' contribution to the usage of "the kingdom of God" and "the kingdom of Heaven" is noteworthy:

> The kingdom of heaven or the kingdom of God is the central theme of Jesus' preaching according to the Synoptic Gospels. While Matthew, who addresses himself to the Jews, speaks for the most part of "the kingdom of heaven," Mark and Luke speak of "the kingdom of God", which has the same meaning as "the kingdom of heaven," but was more intelligible to non-Jews. The use of "Kingdom of Heaven" in Matthew is certainly due to the tendency in Judaism to avoid the direct use of the name of God.[6]

"The kingdom of God" occurs four times in Matthew (12:28; 19:24; 21:31; 21:43), fourteen times in Mark, thirty-two times in Luke, twice in John (3:3, 5), six times in Acts, eight times in Paul, once in Revelation (12:10).[7] Thus, the phrase "the kingdom of God" appears 77 times in the New Testament Canon. The "kingdom of God" appears 53 times in the New Testament Gospels.[8] However, the synonymous phrase, "kingdom of heaven," appears 32 times in

---

[4] Caragounis, "Kingdom of God/Kingdom of Heaven," 417.

[5] Ladd, "Kingdom of Christ, God, Heaven, 607.

[6] H. Ridderbos, "Kingdom of God, Kingdom of Heaven," in *New Bible Dictionary: Second Edition* ed. J. D. Douglas (Wheaton: Tyndale House Publishers Inc., 1982), 656.

[7] Ladd, "Kingdom of Christ, God, Heaven, 607.

[8] *What was the Message of Jesus? What was the Core of Jesus' Preaching?* http://www.patheos.com/blogs/markdroberts/2011/05/05/what-was-the-core-of-jesus-preaching/ (Accessed on May 28, 2013).

the Gospel of Matthew.[9] The frequency of the phrase "kingdom of God" and "the kingdom of Heaven[s]" in the New Testament indicate the extreme significance it has in the life of humanity—God's creation in his own image (Gen. 1:26-27).

The King of "the Kingdom of God"

God is King, enthroned over, not in or among, the affairs of his creation.[10]

Gaffin Jr. elaborates:

> The phrase "the Kingdom of God" does not occur in the Old Testament. But the notions of God as king and of His kingly rule are pervasive. There are various dimensions to his kingship. As the maker and sustainer of all that exists, He is the great King over all the earth. (Ps. 47:2), and His kingdom rules over all the (Ps. 103:19); His kingly control equally encompasses the past, present and future (Your kingdom is an everlasting kingdom, and your dominion endures through all generations, Ps. 145:13; see Providence, Sovereignty of God.[11]

God is eternal King of His eternal kingdom. His kingdom dominates all spiritual and earthly kingdoms, dominions, and thrones. "The biblical idea of God's sovereignty includes all that is involved in the divine kingship—ownership (all things are God's), authority (expression of His own character as righteous and holy love), and control (the master of His universe)."[12] As King of the kingdom of

---

[9] Ibid.,

[10] Ian B. Johnson, "God is King: God's Sovereignty; His Eternal Kingdom," christian-oneness.org/about-God/chapter6.html. (Accessed June 2, 2013).

[11] R. B. Gaffin Jr. "Kingdom of God," in *New Dictionary of Theology,* ed. Sinclair B. Ferguson (Downers Grove: InterVarsity Press, 1988), 367.

[12] D. Macleod, "Sovereignty of God," in *New Dictionary of Theology,"* ed. Sinclair B. Ferguson (Downers Grove: InterVarsity Press, 1988).

God His kingship transcends all ages and times, all nations including Israel, creation, and all events according to His sovereignty. His kingdom has no boundaries, nor limitations to space and time. The King of glory is the king of His Kingdom. His kingship and sovereignty are interrelated in His economy.

The Message of "the Kingdom of God"

"In those days came John the Baptist, preaching in the wilderness of Judea, And saying, Repent ye: for the kingdom of heaven is at hand" (Matt. 3:1-2). "Now after that John was put into prison, Jesus came into Galilee, preaching the gospel of the kingdom of God, And saying, The time is fulfilled, and the kingdom of God is at hand: repent ye, and believe the gospel" (Mark 1: 14-15). The message of "the kingdom of God" elicits a positive response—a believing faith in the gospel of "the kingdom of God"—a sincere penitence, with genuine repentance and remorse of sin of rebellion and disobedience toward God. The message unfolds God's passionate and longing love that seeks to bring to Himself wayward, depraved, and hopeless humanity to cleave to His open arms for perpetual communion—the heartbeat of God.

The message of the Kingdom is hope to the hopeless; it elaborates the foreknowledge of God about the fall of humanity, His divine provision through His only Son Jesus Christ, and the eternal damnation of arch-enemy Satan and all his subjects (spirit beings and human beings).

The Partakers of "the Kingdom of God"

Partakers of the kingdom of God are those born of God (John 1:13)—a mystery that takes intentional and exclusive faith in Jesus Christ to comprehend. Thus, partakers of the kingdom of God respond affirmatively to the message of the Kingdom with genuine repentance and remorse, and accept the indescribable gift of the Father's love through explicit faith in his Son Jesus Christ (John 1:10-13; 3:16; Rom. 5:6-8; I John 5:1-12).

The Condition to Partake in "the Kingdom of God"

"Verily, verily, I say unto thee, except a man be born again, he cannot see the kingdom of God" (John 3:3). I assume Nicodemus nearly fainted with astonishment the words of Jesus Christ. It was strange for a living being to be born again. Nicodemus was right in human estimation, but that proved his naivety in the things of God.

Philipps add an interesting exposition of this discourse;

> In effect he was saying this to Nicodemus: Except you respond to what John's baptism stood for—repentance; except you are, so to speak, "born of water"; except you come by way of repentance; except you respond to what I stand for, regeneration; except you are "born of the Spirit," you cannot enter the kingdom of God. The challenge was this—no John, no Jesus. No repentance and no regeneration mean no rebirth, and apart from rebirth the kingdom of heaven is closed to you.[13]

Thus, the nationality of Nicodemus as a Jew, his religious education as a Pharisee and a member of the Jewish supreme council did not satisfy the condition to partake the kingdom of God. Human achievements without being born by the Spirit of God through faith in the Son of God do not meet the condition to partake in the kingdom of God.

Human invented philosophies attempt to suppress the biblical truth of the condition to become partakers of the kingdom of God because of either naivety in Christology, self indulgence based on nationality, self-aggrandizing based on wealth, political platform, scholastics, societal status, or being a leader of a particular religious organization.

"The first condition is to "repent and believe the gospel" (*see* Repentance; Matt. 4:17) with a childlike faith.[14]—a strong con-

---

[13] John Phillips, *Exploring the Gospel of John: An Expository Commentary* (Grand Rapids: Kregel, 1989), 67.

[14] Caragounis, "Kingdom of God/Kingdom of Heaven," 424.

viction as a sinner in need of a Savior, heart-felt remorse, genuine repentance, reverenced recognition, and sincere faith in Jesus Christ. A graphic illustration of this humble approach was demonstrated by one of the malefactors hanged with Jesus Christ (Luke 23:39-43). In spite of the frequency and enormity of crimes he had committed that warranted his crucifixion as a hardened criminal, the aforementioned repentant sinner became a partaker of the kingdom of God even at the point of death because he met the theological and biblical conditions to partake the kingdom of God.

Johnson prudently affirms that "it is not outward religiosity or public profession that one is doing God's will which places one in the Kingdom, but actually putting God's will first."[15] If outward religiosity and other rituals are requisite to enter into the kingdom of God then the religious leaders in the time of Jesus Christ should not have been at logger heads with Him. Hence, unambiguous and unreserved submission to Jesus Christ as personal Lord and Savior fulfills the condition to partake in the Kingdom of God.

---

[15] Ian B. Johnson, "God is King: The Kingdom of God is Where God is King, not in word, but in power,"christian-oneness.org/about-God/chapter6.html (Accessed on July 20, 2013).

CHAPTER 2

THE NATURE OF "THE KINGDOM OF GOD"

"The Kingdom of God" is God's Rule and Reign

"The "kingdom of God" means primarily the rule of God, the divine kingly authority."[16] There is a sharp dichotomy between God's rule, and other human kings and their reign. "In Old Testament usage, the Hebrew word *malekut,* like *baselelia,* carries primarily the abstract rather than the concrete meaning, thus a king's reign is frequently dated by the phrase "in the…year of this *malekut,*" i.e., of his reign (I Chr. 26:31; Dan. 1:1)."[17] The rule and reign of human kings are very temporal. Their rule has geographical boundaries—limited to specific territories. "But when *malekut* is used of God, it almost always refers to his authority or his rule as the heavenly King. See Pss. 22:28; 103:19; 145:11, 13; Obad. 21; Dan. 6:26."[18] The kingly authority of God transcends time and space.

"In the New Testament, the kingdom of God is the divine authority and the rule given by the Father to the Son (Luke 22:29), Christ will exercise this rule until he has subdued all that is hostile to God."[19] Hostile kingdoms are those that are backed by Satanic and

---

[16] Ladd, "Kingdom of Christ, God, Heaven,"608.

[17] Ibid.

[18] Ibid.

[19] Ibid.

human authority—they are in perpetual conflict and confrontation with the kingdom of God. While the King of the kingdom of God gathers and brings in the sheaves (humanity) and protects them, the assailing kingdoms are indignantly burned with fierce violence to thwart and nullify the plan of the King for His subjects.

"The Kingdom, which men must receive with childlike simplicity (Mark 10:15; Matt. 19:14; Luke 18:17), which men must seek (Matt. 6:33; Luke 12:31), which Christ will give to his disciples (Luke 22:29); is the divine rule."[20] Contrary to other kingdoms that impose authority through violence, torture, and intimidation, the kingdom of God is received voluntarily with strong conviction of a critical need of Jesus Christ as Lord, Savior, and King.

"The Kingdom of God" is Soteriological

"The object of the divine rule is the redemption of men and their deliverance from the powers of evil."[21] Ladd further advocates that "the kingdom of God is the reign of God in Christ destroying all that is hostile to the divine rule,"[22] and saving those under the domain of the arch enemy (Satan) of humanity and God. "God allows Christ to stand in our place, taking our guilt upon himself, so that his righteousness won by obedience upon the cross might become ours."[23] "For he hath made him to be sin for us, who knew no sin; that we might be made the righteousness of God in him" (II Cor. 5:21). "Christ became the substitute—the one who went to the Cross of Calvary to be crucified on behalf of sinful humanity."[24] Adam and Eve became slaves to Satan (Rom. 6:16) as a result of their voluntary disobedience to the word of God (Gen. 3:1-13). God in His agape love sent His only Son Jesus Christ to pay the penalty of the sin of humanity, and deliver Satan-enslaved humanity from the torments and tyranny of Satan, sin, and death.

---

[20] Ibid.

[21] Ibid.

[22] Ibid.

[23] Alister E. McGrath, *Christian Theology: An Introduction*, Fourth Edition (Malden: Blackwell Publishing, 2007), 341.

[24] Ibid., 340.

"The *Christus victor* approach to the death and resurrection of Christ lays considerable emphasis upon the notion of Christ's victory over forces which enslaved humanity, such as, satanic oppression, evil spirits, fear of death, or the power of sin."[25] The salvific program is the bedrock of the kingdom of God. Thus, the King of all kings, and the Lord of all lords (Rev. 17:14; 19:16) perpetually seeks "to save that which was lost" (Luke 19:10) in order to establish the kingdom of God in the penitent sinners through their faith in Christ Jesus. By the power of His blood, the Savior cleanses those who believe in Him from all the tyranny of sin and its devastating consequence—death.

The Mystery of "the Kingdom of God"

"The presence of the Kingdom in history is a mystery."[26] As was His custom to speak in parables, one day Jesus Christ taught about the parable of the sower. He told His disciples "Unto you it is given to know the mystery of the kingdom of God: but unto them that are without, all these things are done in parables" (Mark 4:11). Ladd defines mystery as "a divine purpose hidden for long ages but finally revealed."[27] There is a sharp dichotomy between mystery and magic. In this context mystery is the interpretation of biblical truth that convicts sinners and brings them under the Cross with remorse, penitence, and faith in Christ. Magic is Satan-backed trick that spontaneously arouses its audiences' attention with false hope and stirs their enthusiasm to remain captives to Satan and worldly enticements. The mysterious God is the ultimate initiator and revealer of mysteries.

The Imminence of "the Kingdom of God"

"The claim that the kingdom of God had arrived in Jesus' person and that it consisted of, or at least was active in, driving out demons

---

[25] Ibid., 354.
[26] Ladd, "Kingdom of Christ, God, Heaven," 609.
[27] Ibid.

is hardly a satisfactory answer to the three questions regarding the essence, the arrival, and the relation of the kingdom of God to Jesus' person and work."[28] In one of His usual confrontations with evil spirits and human assailants (the scribes and Pharisees), Jesus was accused of casting "out devils through Beelzebub the chief of the devils" (Luke 11: 15). The false thoughts of the attackers of Christ moved Him to rebuke them with poignant spiritual truth (Luke 11:16-20.)

"When the King came to earth as man, the Kingdom followed him wherever he went, and the enemies of the Kingdom could not stand in his presence."[29] They trapped him even in his speech, his exorcism, and in all his movements. They could not stand him in all spheres. He triumphed over all forces and agents of Satan, evil, and death—all with the goal to establish the kingdom of God in the life of humanity. This battle between God and Satanic forces authenticates the biblical truth that supports the essence, the arrival and the relation of the kingdom of God to the person and the work of Jesus Christ. Throughout His ministry, Jesus exorcized by casting out devils and rendering captives healed and free to become partakers of the Kingdom through their faith in Him (Mark 1:32-34).

"Because the dynamic power of God's reign has invaded this evil age, it has created a present spiritual realm in which the blessings of God's reign are experience."[30] Though Jesus disarmed and triumphed over satanic agents and forces (Col. 2:15), not all human beings are subjects or partakers of the kingdom of God. The theological and biblical condition to partake in the blessing in the kingdom of God is faith in Jesus Christ (John 3:16). "Though the redeemed have already been delivered from the power of darkness and brought into the kingdom of Christ (Col. 1:13),"[31] those who voluntarily reject the Lordship of Jesus Christ are still under satanic oppression as his captives.

---

[28] Caragounis, "Kingdom of God/Kingdom of Heaven," 423.

[29] Ian B. Johnson, God is King: The Kingdom then Came to Earth in the Person of Its King," christian-oneness.org/about-God/chapter6html (Accessed on August 12, 2013).

[30] Ladd, "Kingdom of Christ, God, Heaven," 610.

[31] Ibid.

"The Kingdom of God" is Eschatological

"In this age, partakers of the Kingdom will experience suffering (II Thess. 1:5) and tribulations (Acts 14:22), but God will rescue them from every evil and save them for his heavenly kingdom (II Tim. 4:18)."[32] The wisest and best decision a human being would ever make on this sin polluted earth is receiving Christ Jesus as personal Lord and Savior—the first step to transition from the kingdom of destruction, darkness, and death into the blessed kingdom of God (Matt. 7:13-14). At the same time, this Spirit-led decision is accompanied by many traumatic but temporal challenges that sometimes lead to martyrdom for the sake of Christ and His cause.

"In the Gospels, eschatological salvation is described as entrance into the kingdom of God (Mark 9:47; 10:24), into the age to come (Mark 10:30), and into eternal life (Mark 9:45; 10:17, 30; Matt 25:46)."[33] The sequence of this historical event conveys a biblical truth that in spite of the magnitude of accompanied persecutions, the unparalleled climax is eternal life in Christ Jesus.

Ladd shares further insights on this:

> The consummation of the kingdom requires the coming of the Son of man in glory. Satan will be destroyed (Matt. 25:41), the dead in Christ raised in incorruptible bodies (I Cor. 1542-50) which are no longer capable of death (Luke 20: 35-36) to inherit the kingdom of God (I Cor. 15:50; Matt. 25:34). Before his death Jesus promised his disciples renewed fellowship in the new order (Matt. 26:29) when they would share both his fellowship and his authority to rule (Luke 22:29-30).[34]

At the divinely appointed time, Jesus Christ who triumphed over satanic forces and agents through His death and resurrection (Col.

---

[32] Ibid.

[33] Ibid.

[34] Ibid.

2:15) will finally destroy the destroyer. Jesus implored His disciples to continue in their unwavering faith in the Godhead, even though His departure invited situations of desolation and abandonment; expose the first century disciples to hostility and outrageous persecutions, Jesus promised to come back in the future (a date and time not known by any human being (Acts 1:7), and transport His disciples (partakers of the kingdom of God) to be with Him till the end of the age. It is incumbent to state that not only the first century believers in Christ, but throughout all generations everyone who accepts the glorious invitation of the Father and come to Him by faith through His Son Jesus Christ would enjoy eternity with the Godhead.

"The Kingdom of God" is Dynamic

"Jesus' conception of the kingdom of God had continuity with the OT promise sharing certain features with apocalyptic Judaism, particularly Daniel; but Jesus' conception went beyond the others in certain important aspects."[35] Johnson posits that; "the kingdom of God appeared to have passed through five distinct periods with the first period running from before Creation to the creation of man."[36] "During that time God had not created human beings, so it is convincing that God's reign was not shared with any creature. The second brief period began when God created Adam and Eve (Gen. 1:26-30),"[37] prior to the fatal fall of humanity. "The third period began when Adam and Eve sinned"[38] against God by voluntarily violating God's command *(Gen. 2:17)*. However, the serpent was able to win the whims and caprice of Adam and Eve through its usual subtle inclination and approach to the first couple (Gen. 3:1-13). As a result of the weakness and disobedience of Adam and Eve, the serpent held them as its subjects and captives. Thus, the kingdom of God was divided with God's rule over those who obey

---

[35] Caragounis, "Kingdom of God/Kingdom of Heaven," 420.

[36] Ian B. Johnson, "God is King: God's Kingdom is Eternal and Unchanging, but Appears to us to Vary," christian-oneness.org/about-Godchapter6.html (Accessed August 12, 2013).

[37] Ibid.

[38] Ibid.

His word as against the opposing satanic rule over the disobedient (Rom. 6:16).

"The fourth period surfaced when the King himself was born on earth as a human."[39] "And, behold, thou shalt conceive in thy womb, and bring forth a son, and shalt call his name JESUS...And he shalt reign over the house of Jacob forever; and of his kingdom there shall be no end" (Luke 1:31-33). The kingdom of God was made manifest in the preaching and teaching of Jesus Christ (Matt. 13:47-50) amidst forgiveness of sin and condemnation to death (John 8:1-11), casting out devils, healing the sick, cleansing the lepers (Matt.10:8), and raising the dead (John 11:39-44). "After King Jesus physically left the earth, he sent the Holy Spirit that could live in everyone who believes in Him"[40] to advance the Kingdom of God on earth. To fulfill the word spoken by the prophet Joel (Joel 2:28-29), the Spirit of God came upon the one hundred and twenty believers in the upper room ten days after His ascension (Acts 2: 1-4). On that day alone three thousand believers were added to the subjects of the kingdom (Acts 2:41).

"The fifth period of the kingdom is the harvest, the time of judgment which leads out of time into eternity—a time that God's Kingdom will crush and replace all kingdoms on this earth (Dan. 2:35, 44-45; Rev. 11:15)."[41] "When the Son of man comes in his glory, he will sit on the throne of judgment (Matt. 25:31-35)."[42] The sovereign kingship of God is beyond creation and transcends the end of the age, and it prevails over all human biases and prejudices through faith in the Son of God.

Caragounis expands Jesus' concept of the kingdom of God with the following points:

1. The kingdom of God is primarily dynamic rather than geographical entity.

---

[39] Ibid.

[40] Ibid.

[41] Ibid.

[42] Ladd, "The Kingdom of Christ, God, Heaven,"609.

2. The kingdom of God is connected with the destiny of the Son of man.

3. Entrance into the kingdom of God is not based on the covenant or confined to Jewish participation.

4. In apocalypticism the kingdom of God is vague future hope, in Jesus it is definite and imminent, in fact it demands immediate response.[43]

But, it is equally important to emphasize that God is "not willing that any should perish, but that all should come to repentance" (2 Pet. 3:9) and partake in the kingdom of God.

Ladd also argues that; "Jesus separated the present and future eschatological coming of the Kingdom at the end of the age."[44] Rick Love affirms that; "this understanding of the present and future dimensions of the kingdom of God sets forth what theologians refer to as the eschatological structure of the whole Bible."[45] Thus, the message of the Kingdom requires immediate and positive response to accept its unbiased and open-to-all invitation into the Kingdom through faith in Christ Jesus.

---

[43] Caragounis, "Kingdom of God/Kingdom of Heaven," 420.

[44] Ladd, "Kingdom of Christ, God, Heaven,"609.

[45] Rick Love, *Muslims, Magic and the Kingdom of God* (Pasadena: William Carey Library, 2000), 42-43.

CHAPTER 3

THE NATURE OF SPIRITUAL WARFARE

The Meaning of Spiritual Warfare

From a Christian perspective, spiritual warfare is the cosmic war of good versus evil.[46] The "good" in this context means things that are approved and pleasing to God (Gen. 1:31), and the "evil" are things that are disapproved and displeasing to God (John 3:19). The "good" referred to is not the popular slogan "freedom of speech"—to talk in any manner without an iota of prudence, and courtesy, "freedom to worship"—worship either idols or gods (spirits, human beings, or wealth), "freedom to marry or engage in same sex abhorring relationships"—acquiescence, approval, and promotion of homosexuality, lesbianism, and other seemingly freedom of choice that are not freedom in themselves but are heavy yokes and shackles of servitude in the lives of captives of Satan.

"Spiritual Warfare is that conflict being waged in the invisible, spiritual realm that is being manifest in the visible, physical realm."[47] The ongoing conflicts in marriages, families, churches, communities, nations, etc., are vivid manifestations of spiritual warfare.

---

[46] *What is Spiritual Warfare? A Definition of Spiritual Warfare*, http://www.battlefocused.org/articles/what-is-spiritual-warfare/ (Accessed on August 17, 2013).

[47] Tony Evans, *The Battle is the Lord's: Waging Victorious Spiritual Warfare* (Chicago: Moody Publishers, 1998), 18.

There is no bunker or foxhole that you crawl into that will shield you from the effects of this cosmic battle between the forces of God and the forces of Satan."[48] Human beings are targets of satanic affliction.

The reality of spiritual warfare cannot be underestimated. It is actually against a controlled system of power and influence by the arch enemy Satan in the heavenly realms through those who succumb to his rebellious authority, power, and dominion. As a murderer, liar, and the father of all liars (John 8:44) Satan manipulates spiritual beings, human beings, human authorities (such as governments, business owners, wealthy people and people of influence) to thwart the plan of God. Satan never relents, nor does he ever break in his proceedings to opposition to the plan of God to redeem the "cosmos" from his control. "…[A]s a roaring lion…seeking who he may devour" (I Pet. 5:8), Satan is at war all day and all night with humanity especially partakers of the kingdom of God.

Though a defeated foe (Col. 2:15), Satan never gets tired of fighting a lost battle. Satan is perpetually prone "to steal, and to kill, and to destroy" (John 10:10). The reality and evil intention of Satan against God and His Kingdom supports the advocacy of the meaning of spiritual warfare. It is waged in the spiritual realm and made manifest in the physical through diversity of events in the world.

The Parties Involved in Spiritual Warfare

The number of personalities involved in this warfare is many. They are; the forces of Satan (composed of fallen angels and human agents) against God along with His angels and His children. Who is God? Who is Satan? Who are angels? Who are fallen angels? Who are human beings? And, who are children of God?

"God is indescribable because humans are finite and God is infinite."[49] Human beings, as finite as we are, can never fully understand the nature of God.

---

[48] Ibid.,

[49] Millard J. Erickson, *Christian Theology, Second Edition* (Grand Rapids: Baker Academy, 2009), 178.

Saucy's argument on this issue is classic:

> According to the Scriptures, God is known only through His self-revelation. Apart from his initiative in disclosing himself God could not be known by man. Human attempts to reason to God in various means, including the so-called proofs of, God while they can provide evidence for the need of a god, do not yet attain to the knowledge of the true God (cf. I Cor. 1:21a). Limited to the realm of creation, whether external nature or human subjective experience, man is incapable of reasoning to a valid knowledge of the transcendent Creator.[50]

God chooses to reveal Himself to humans according to His grace and mercies. Centuries and decades of research by scientists in all disciplines, liberal theologians, and other philosophers would not suffice in their quest to know who God really is. "Finitude cannot comprehend infinity."[51] Though the incomprehensible God reveals Himself to humans, it does not mean that man is capable of knowing who God is in totality.

The God of Scripture is a personal Being (Isa. 42:8). "Nowhere is the personhood of God more evident than in his biblical description of the Father—Jesus constantly spoke of God as "my Father," "your Father," and "the heavenly Father.""[52] Furthermore, "the biblical concept of the personhood of God refutes all abstract philosophical ideas of God as merely First Cause and pantheistic concepts."[53] As a Creator, Revealer, Cross-Cultural-Communicator, his personhood subjugates and negates all human ideas. God is not a wind, an air, a fire, breath, or any definition that usurps His Personhood.

God as Spirit Being denies false pretence—in the form of statues, images, shrines, objects, buildings, geographical location, in some

---

[50] R. Saucy, "God, Doctrine of," in *Evangelical Dictionary of Theology* ed. Walter E. Elwell (Grand Rapids: Baker Books, 1999), 459.

[51] Ibid., 460.

[52] Ibid., 461.

[53] Ibid.

specific humans, time and space. God is neither under the control of any human being, nor is He restricted to any particular place in a given time. "In His holiness God is the transcendent Deity."[54] His holiness is not defined by human finite estimation. God did not assume, earn, or work for holiness. Rather, He is who He is before time and through eternity (Ps. 90:2).

"Crucial to the biblical doctrine of God is His Trinitarian nature—a term used to designate the threefold manifestation of the One God as Father, Son, and Holy Spirit."[55] Though the word or term "trinity" is not found in the Bible, the interpretation is very vivid.

Saucy has this to say about the "Trinity":

> The doctrine of the Trinity flows from the self-revelation of God in biblical salvation history. As the one God successfully reveals himself in his saving action in the Son and the Holy Spirit, each is recognized as God himself in personal manifestation. It is thus in the fullness of NT revelation that the doctrine of the Trinity is seen most clearly. God is one (Gal 3:20; James 2:19), but the Son (John 1:1; 14:9; Col.2:9), and the Spirit (Acts 5:3-4; I Cor. 3;16) are also fully God.[56]

The Trinity is clearly revealed in the salvific plan of God. Thus, the Father gave His only Son Jesus Christ (John 3:16), as a demonstration of God's love (Rom. 5:8), to pay the penalty of sin and justification for depraved humanity through His death and resurrection (Rom. 4:25). The Holy Spirit is the Dispenser of this unmerited favor of God to wayward humanity through conviction of sin (John 16:8-9), confession of sin (I John 1:9), confession of Jesus as Lord (Rom. 10:9-10), through adoption of believers in Christ into the family of God (Rom. 8:15-16), and helper to the subjects of the kingdom of God in their daily lives in Christ (John 16:5-15).

---

[54] Ibid.

[55] Ibid.

[56] Ibid., 462.

Who is Satan? "First and foremost Satan is not equal to the Most High God.[57] Rather, Satan is an ancient and extremely treacherous foe"[58] of God (his Creator) and humanity. "While references to Satan are not as common in the Old Testament as they are in the New, Satan is mentioned several times: once in I Chronicles, fourteen times in Job 1 and 2, once in Psalm 109:6, and three times in Zechariah 3:1-2."[59] Satan's insolence and fruitless effort to usurp the authority and power of God, and his subsequent warfare against God and God's salvific plan for humanity do not put Satan at parallel with the self-existing God. "Yea, before the day was I am he" (Isa. 43:13a). Rather, "Satan (the Hebrew word for adversary), the devil, is a high angelic creature who, before the creation of the human race, rebelled against the Creator and became the chief antagonist of God and man."[60] "Satan is the principle name of the devil, although he was first named "Lucifer" before he rebelled against God in the pre-creation universe, and the slanderer of men to God and of God to men."[61] "The word Satan is used about fifty-five times in the New Testament, and devil is used about thirty-five times.[62] To deny the reality and the mission of the devil is to deny God and His Word.

Kurt Koch's biblical exposure of the devil is noteworthy;

> The devil is many-sided and versatile demagogue. To the psychologist he says, "I will give you new knowledge and understanding." He confronts the religionist and the moralist with a musk of integrity and promises them the very help from heaven. And finally to

---

[57] *What is Spiritual Warfare? Alternative viewpoints in teaching Spiritual Warfare: Dualism*, http://www.battlefocused.org/articles/what-is-spiritual-warfare/ (Accessed on August 15, 2013).

[58] Francis Frangipane, *The Three Battlegrounds: An In-depth View of Three Arenas of Spiritual Warfare: The Mind, the Church and the Heavenly Places* (Cedar Rapids: Arrow Publications Inc., 2012), 7.

[59] Ed Murphy, *The Handbook for Spiritual Warfare* (Tennessee: Thomas Nelson Inc., 2003), 18-19.

[60] Merrill F. Unger, "Satan," in *Evangelical Dictionary of Theology*, ed. Walter A. Elwell (Grand Rapids: Baker Books, 1999), 972.

[61] Frangipane, *The Three Battlegrounds*, 169.

[62] Evans, *The Battle is the Lord's*, 157.

the rationalist and the liberalist he says, "I am not there.I do not exist. ." The devil is a skilful strategist. He is the master of every tactic of the battlefield. He befogs the front. He hides behind a camouflage of empty religious talk. He operates through the use of the latest scientific method. He successfully launches his arguments on the social and humane plane. And his main aim is to deceive, to entice, and to ensnare his victims.[63]

The reality of the devil cannot be overruled by any theory or discovery. His works are made manifest in the lives of depraved humanity among Jews and Gentiles, the rich and the poor, the societal elite and the outcast, and both men and women. He capitalizes on subtle character to deceive his adherents of his nonexistence. He roams about with his demons to lure the ignorant and the arrogant, capture them in his traps, and works through them to intensify the ongoing spiritual battle against the advancement of the kingdom of God.

"Once created as God's most gifted and beautiful supernatural being, Satan abused his authority and then led a rebellion against Yahweh...and his final destruction is decreed."[64] Though the devil is at work through deception, intimidation, distortion of the truth and diverse strategies to revamp the advancement of the kingdom of God a divine appointed time is set for his perpetual torture and torment. Satan's rebellion against God amounts to nothing as compared with the doom and destruction that awaits him and his allies. "Jesus' complete defeat of the Devil and his demons is expected in the eschaton."[65] The end of Satan is everlasting agonized torments—a divine punitive action for his evil thought, rebellious deeds, crafty persuasion in paralyzing the faith of some believers in Christ, and his dominion over his subjects (unbelievers in Christ).

---

[63] Kurt Koch, *The Devil's Alphabet* (Grand Rapids: Kregel Publications, 1971), 7.

[64] Gerald R. McDermott, *God's Rivals: Why Has God Allowed Different Religions?* (Downers Grove: IVP Academic, 2007), 57.

[65] Graham H. Twelftree, "Demons, Devil, Satan," in *Dictionary of Jesus and the Gospels:* ed. Joel B. Green (Downers Grove: InterVarsity Press, 1992), 163.

Who are angels? "According to the Gospels, angels are spirit beings who serve God, particularly in connection with Jesus' work of proclaiming and establishing the kingdom of God."[66] Bromiley says; "angels are God's messengers or ambassadors, they belong to his divinely court and service, and their mission in heaven is to praise God."[67] The narration of the birth of Christ (Luke 1:26-36), Jesus' temptation in the wilderness by Satan (Luke 4:1-13), at the resurrection of Jesus Christ (Matt.28:2-7), and angels will come with Jesus when he returns in great glory (Matt. 24:31-32) are few examples that demonstrate their service to God.

"In second century Christianity, attempts were made to describe both Christ and the Holy Spirit in angelic terms; but the New Testament picture of a Christ distinguished from, and infinitely superior to, all other powers prevailed (Col. 1:16; Heb. 1:4-5)."[68] As discussed earlier in this book, the Trinity is God the Father, the Son, and the Holy Spirit. Any beings (spiritual and physical) are creatures, and therefore not parallel to the Godhead. Kearsley advocates that the term angel simply means 'messenger' (Heb. *mal'ak,* Gk. *angelos).*[69] As part of creation angels are messengers of the God of creation. Therefore, all heretical attempts or descriptions to de-infinite the finite God proves futile.

Who is "the angel of the Lord"? In the OT and NT the angel of the Lord *(mal'ak yhwh)* is represented as acting on behalf of the nation of Israel as well as individuals.[70]

Davidson's exposition of "the angel of the Lord" is noteworthy:

> In the OT the phrase "the Angel of the Lord" occurs some sixty times. This angel is a special servant of

---

[66] Maxwell J. Davidson, "Angels," in *Dictionary of Jesus and the Gospels,* ed. Joel B. Green (Downers Grove: InterVarsity Press, 1992), 8.

[67] Geoffrey W. Bromiley, "Angel," in *Evangelical Dictionary of Theology,* ed. Walter A. Elwell (Grand Rapids: Baker Books, 1999), 46.

[68] R. Kearsley, "Angels," in *New Dictionary of Theology,* ed. Sinclair B. Ferguson (Downers Grove: InterVarsity Press, 1988), 21.

[69] Ibid., 20.

[70] Thomas E. McComiskey, "Angel of the Lord," in *Evangelical Dictionary of Theology,* ed. Walter A. Elwell (Grand Rapids: Baker Books, 1999), 47.

Yahweh who helps accomplish God's will among his people. Thus he appears to Moses at the burning bush (Ex. 3:2), opposed Balaam (Num. 22:22-35) and encouraged Gideon (Judg. 6:11-16). He is said to have caused death among Israel's enemies (2 Kings 19:35) and in Israel itself (I Chron. 21:14-15), though he usually comes to the aid of God's people (Ex. 14:19; Judg. 2:1; I Kings 19:7; Ps.34:7).[71]

The clear distinction between "angels" and "the angel of the Lord" should not be underemphasized based on their respective designations or how they are addressed and

their respective assignments. On the flipside, "the angel of the Lord" is not the pre-incarnate appearance of Jesus Christ. There is no substantial evidence to authenticate this hollow argument. Rather, "the angel of the Lord" is a self-manifestation of Yahweh in a form that would communicate his immanence and direct concern to those to whom he ministered."[72] The sovereign God manifests Himself in any way He finds fitting to accomplish His cause for His own pleasure. Any human interpretation (philosophy, theory, or conclusion) to derail from the Scriptures of the Creator God is heresy, unfounded, baseless, blasphemous, and deceptive.

Who are fallen angels? The prophet Isaiah conveys a concise insight that helps to answer this question:

> How art thou fallen from heaven, O Lucifer, son of the morning! How art thou cut down to the ground, which didst weaken the nations! For thou hast said in thine heart, I will ascend into heaven, I will exalt my throne above the stars of God: I will sit also upon the mount of the congregation, in the sides of the north: I will ascend above the heights of the clouds; I will be like the most High. Yet thou shalt be brought down to hell, to the sides of the pit. (Isa. 14:12-15)

---

[71] Davidson, "The Angel of the Lord," 9.
[72] McComiskey, "Angel of the Lord," 48.

"In his rebellious thought Satan, also known as Lucifer, led about one third of the angels against God."[73] Satan aspired to ascend and live beyond the throne of God, to lavish himself with self-claimed titles, to clothe himself with splendor, and to carry out his deadly mission along with his agents. Instead, God cast Satan down with the angels who possessed similar evil thoughts of usurpation (Prov. 16:18). This evil contingent of rebellious angels, including their chief Lucifer, is classified as "the fallen angels."

Who are human beings?

> And God made the beast of the earth after its kind, and cattle after their kind, and everything that creepeth upon the earth after its kind: and God saw that it was good. And God said, Let us make man in our image, after our likeness: and let them have dominion over the fish of the sea, and over the fowl of the air, and over every creeping thing that creepeth upon the earth. So God created man in his own image, in the image of God created he him; male and female created hethem. (Gen. 1:25-17)

My concern under this subsection is to prove beyond reasonable doubt, with substantial biblical and theological argument, that humanity did not evolve from monkeys and apes as deceitfully and erroneously taught by evolution scientists. The Scripture of the Creator God adequately proves that beasts (including monkeys and apes), and cattle of all kinds were created by God not after the image of God but after its kind (vs. 25). They are classified by the Creator as beasts. Re-defining this class of creation is baseless, heretic, and unbiblical. Beasts will continue to be beasts until the end of the age. In the creation of humanity the Creator mentions that in His image (*imago Dei*) and in the likeness of the Creator God He created

---

[73] *The Spiritual War: Introduction to Spiritual Warfare—When did Spiritual Warfare Begin?* http://www.truthnet.org/Spiritual-warfare/1SpiritualWarfare/Spiritual-warfare.htm (Accessed on August 17, 2013).

them (male and female) to dominate all beasts (including monkeys and apes), on the earth, and fish in the sea and birds in the air (vss. 26-27). Hence, human beings are created beings in the image of God. "And God blessed them, and God said unto them, Be fruitful, and multiply" (Gen. 1:28a). It is therefore, prudent to advocate that every human being (both dead and alive) on the face of the earth is a descendant of Adam and Eve and not apes in any sense.

Unfortunately, the first human beings (Adam and Eve) created by God in His image and likeness fell prey to the serpent's deceptiveness based on their freewill (Gen. 3: 1-14). As a result of their blatant refusal to reject the serpent's crafty enticement, the first parents fatally fell from God's grace. Hence, all human beings "...have sinned, and come short of the glory of God" (Rom. 3:23). They voluntarily chose to disobey the Creator God and instead obeyed the creature. This act of disobedience to God's command creeps through the human race from generation to generation.

The final question concerning those involved in spiritual warfare is, "Who are children of God?" As shared in the preceding chapter, through the disobedience of Adam and Eve every human being is depraved and corrupt. But the loving and caring God foreknew the disobedience of Adam and Eve so He made provision for atonement by His Son Jesus Christ through explicit faith (John 3:16). This salvific plan of God is for wayward humanity both Jews and Gentiles who believe in the Son of God (John 3:36). The one true sacrifice of the Son of God forgives, cleanses, justifies, pardons, regenerates, delivers, adopts, and imputes righteousness upon the greatest sinner.

Children of God are those who acknowledge their sinfulness as a result of the fall of Adam and Eve (I John 1:8), recognize their need for the Savior Jesus Christ (Rom. 7:24), accept Him into their lives by faith (I John 5:1), filled with the Holy Spirit (John 20:22; Acts 2:4), and are led by the Spirit of God (Rom. 8:14).

Children of God are people of prayer and fervent faith (Luke 18:1- 8). Additionally, children of God do witness Jesus Christ in the power of the Holy Ghost (Acts 1:8); are more than conquerors in spite of the perpetual spiritual warfare of Satanic forces, the world, and the flesh (Rom. 8:35-39). Even in the midst of escalating persecution faced by children of God (John 16:33), they live lives worthy of God's calling upon them (Eph.4:1) as they walk and labor with the Lord Jesus Christ. They eagerly await the second coming of the Son of God for His Church (I Thess. 4:13-18), and to be with them forever (John 14:1-3).

"Practical god-likeness, which comes from a willing response to the control the Spirit of God, is evidence of being children of God."[74] Despite the enormous cost involved in obeying God's voice (Acts 4:19; 5:29) in this sin-polluted world children of God are perpetually inclined to follow the leading and promptings of the Spirit of God (Rom. 8:14). Children of God hear the voice of Jesus Christ and they follow Him (John 10:27). In spite of what earthly nation or country they belong to, children of God recognize that their ultimate and utmost citizenship is in heaven (Phil. 3:20).

The Origin of Spiritual Warfare

"To understand the origin of the spiritual warfare we have to go back before time into eternity past when God created a body of beings called angels."[75] "The battle is an ancient one."[76] It is not a warfare that was waged by humanity, but by Lucifer. The battle began before God created Adam and Eve.

Embracing and recognizing the undeniable truth that God is the Creator of the universe penetrates and prevails over all impediments that blindfold human comprehension about God as the Sovereign King of His Kingdom. As such, angels are not an exception to God's creation. They are part of creation. If so, then it is relevant to understand that "there is another world, that sits beyond our five senses— the spiritual realm."[77] If angels are created-spiritual-beings then there is sufficient room for humanity to wholly accept the biblical

---

[74] Leslie C. Allen, "Rom. 8:14-17," *Zondervan Bible Commentary*, ed. F. F. Bruce, (Grand Rapids: Zondervan, 2008), 1318-1319.

[75] Evans, *The Battle is of the Lord's*" 36-37.

[76] Paul Alexander, "Spiritual Warfare: The Battle of Ideas, Concepts, and Thoughts," *Enrichment: Enriching and Equipping Spirit-filled Ministers*, Vol. 18, no. 3 (June 2013), 68

[77] Evans, *The Battle is of the Lord's*" 36.

and theological truth that there is a spiritual world in addition to the physical (the cosmic).

Evans conveys an insightful thought:

> Among the angels God created one of them as His special masterpiece—Lucifer the "brilliant" or "the shining" or "star of the morning" also called Satan, devil, accuser of the brethren, and Beelzebub. The spiritual warfare originated in the angelic realm before the creation described in Genesis chapter 1. Thus, the spiritual warfare began with Lucifer's rebellion in company of the angels that are loyal to him against the Creator God in heaven.[78]

God through His prophets has revealed the origin of spiritual warfare. God shows an epitome of Satan through the prophet Ezekiel (Ezek. 28:2). Thus, the origin of spiritual warfare began when Lucifer (also known as Satan, devil, the serpent, the murderer, the slanderer, and the accuser of the brethren) rebelled against God in the spirit realm.

The Battlefield of Spiritual Warfare

Humanity cannot obey God without having a true understanding of God's sovereign power, authority, and rule over creation, and His self eternal existence. This understanding begins in the mind of every individual. Merriam-Webster defines mind "as the element or complex of elements in an individual that feels, perceives, thinks, wills, and especially reasons."[79] The mind chooses to understand, misunderstand, or reject what it hears through the reasoning faculty. In the Garden of Eden, Adam and Eve genuinely knew who God was; but after the serpent had appealed through their ears into their minds, they willingly rejected the word of God by giving their minds over to the serpent (Gen. 3). Thus, the serpent monopolized

---

[78] Ibid., 37.

[79] Merriam-Webster, *Merriam-Webster Collegiate Dictionary: Eleventh Edition* (Springfield: Merriam-Webster Incorporated, 2005), 790.

their carnal mind and won their whims and caprice by aiding them in disobeying God and God's word. The serpent's evil mind was wholeheartedly welcomed by the first couple's (Adam and Eve) evil inclined and evil dominated mind. They became prey to the serpent, and fell from God's grace through their sinful thoughts and deliberate actions against the Creator.

Magdalene's exposition is noteworthy in this discussion:

> The battlefield or realm in which our spiritual warfare takes place is in the mind of every believer in Christ. We wrestle or strive and struggle in our minds against world systems, the flesh or carnal nature, and the devil. The mind encompasses our thoughts (imagination, reasoning, and intellect) as well as our emotions and will. In all these aspects lie the very heart of an individual. By our thoughts and feelings we determine our will and purpose for our lives.[80]

Paul Alexander adds, "Spiritual warfare often takes place in the realm of ideas, concepts, and thoughts."[81] In his doom-trapped and confrontational dialogue with Eve the serpent touched the reasoning faculty of his captor by appealing through her (Eve) ears (Gen. 3:1-5). Eve reasoned in her evil mindset, made an evil decision in her mind, and put the evil thought into action that led to her and Adam's fatal fall from the glory of God (Gen. 3:7-21). A fierce battle went on in their minds and their whole life was manipulated and placed under the servitude of Satan.

Some recent horrible shooting events in the United States of America are erroneously and ignorantly attributed to "boredom" instead of being viewed as the evil plan of the evil-doer Satan (I John 3:3a) through sin dominated minds of those under his domain..

---

[80] *Spiritual Warfare: Battlefield of the Mind: Prepare Your Heart for Warfare*, www.battleinchrist.com (Accessed on August 17, 2013).

[81] Paul Alexander, "Spiritual Warfare: The Battle of Ideas, Concepts, and Thoughts," 67.

NBC News contributor Bill Briggs reports:

Sheer boredom has been cited as a motive in the murders of at least four people in recent years, including the [August 15, 2013] shooting of an Oklahoma College athlete, and leading experts in teen violence say that reason may be quite real in the minds of some youthful killers. A handful of young homicide suspects and convicted killers in recent years told authorities they were pushed by boredom to willfully take a random life. [82]

Then the question is, What "pushed?" or What triggered the so called "push?" Who is the architect of the so-called "boredom" in this context? Answers to the aforementioned questions go on in the mind—thought-life. Both good and bad intentions develop in the mind before it is actualized through other human faculties. The boy who talked with the reporter said, "We were bored and didn't have anything to do, so we decided to kill somebody."[83] They were deceived by the devil to shoot and kill the innocent young man without any justifiable cause. Unfortunately, those who do not believe in God and His word conclude that the murderers killed the Oklahoma College athlete with the baseless reason that the culprits were bored. Here, Satan the evil-doer behind this heinous crime is covered by naïve mentality. Can anybody at all just get up and act inhumanly by destroying the lives of guiltless people and be justified with this flimsy slogan of "boredom". This is a serious spiritual warfare waged against humanity and the plan of the gracious God.

"In 2010, six teenagers fatally stabbed 25-year-old pizza chef Mathew Chew in New London and they told authorities that they did it because they were bored."[84] Ignorantly, those with big and loud microphones (either through wealth, scholastic intricacies,

---

[82] Boredom Blamed for Murders: A True Killing Impulse? http://www.nbcnews.com/health/boredom-blamed-murders-true-killing-impulse-6C10963043 (Accessed on August 22, 2013).

[83] Ibid.,

[84] Ibid.

position in the government, leaders in religious organizations, and other prestigious platforms) cover Satan from his own intentional evil deeds because of lack of knowledge about the ongoing spiritual battle waged by Satan through wicked and crafty schemes. I will never attempt to exaggerate Satan and his rebellious deeds against humanity. Rather I am led by the Spirit of God to expose who the devil is, and his nefarious deeds against God's creation (humanity).

Another atrocious and insane case involved two housemates. One was influenced through his thought-life, killed the other and ate some of the parts of the deceased to satisfy his master Satan. "Alexander Kinyua, 22, told Harford County Judge in Maryland [on August 19, 2013] that he killed his friend with an axe and ate his heart."[85] Cannibalism is sin. Murder is sin. Satan began to sin (I John 3:8). These two foreign students shared a house in Maryland to pursue their respective academic dreams. They shared fellowship for some months if not years prior to the catastrophic murder of Kujoe Adjei-Kodie. Alexander Kinyua from Kenya mercilessly butchered Kujoe Adjei-Kodie and satisfied his deep seated and Satan-backed lust.

What is behind this heinous murder and cannibalism? Is it the usual "boredom," "sleeplessness," or "something" that pushed Kinyua to kill and eat part of the body of Adjei-Kodie? Satan worked tirelessly in the mind of Kinyua, as he did in the case of Cain (Gen. 4). Though Cain did not eat any part of Abel, crafty Satan manipulated the thought-life of Kinyua to eat the heart and brain of his own friend and housemate Adjei-Kodie. Satan dominated the mind of Mr. Alexander Kinyua, and convinced him that it was good to butcher Kujoe Adjei-Kodie. Satan lied to Kinyua by leading him to believe that it was beneficial to have an additional heart in order to excel in his academic pursuit and further help him to become the fastest athlete (in track events) in the history of the cosmic. Kinyua would accomplish this by eating his housemate's heart. Whether the allegations of mine in this chapter are right or wrong, it is Satan the

---

[85] GhanaWeb: Kenyan Cannibal Pleads Guilty to Killing, Eating Ghanaian Mate, http://www.ghheadlines.com/agency/daily-graphic/2013/534124/kenyan-cannibal-pleads-guilty-to-killing—eating-ghanaian-mate—— (Accessed on August 22, 2013)

treacherous old foe of humanity, who dominated the mind of Kinyua to carry out that insane and heinous "kill and eat" crime.

"Jesus Christ was crucified at Golgotha (place of the skull) and to be effective in spiritual warfare warriors must understand that the first field of conflict is the battleground of the mind."[86] The battle of philosophies and concepts begins with verbal and, or non-verbal communications directed straight to the intellect of humanity. The mind is the receptor of all forms of communications either harmonious or hilarious through the five senses. The Holy Scripture says words either kill or give life, "Death and life are in the power of the tongue: and they that love it shall eat the fruit thereof" (Prov. 18:21). Again, Scripture warns the saints of God to "Be not deceived; evil communications corrupt good manners" (I Cor. 15:33). Words are powerful. They are spoken to the mind where the battle begins in the life of humanity. Additionally, man was formed from dust, and the serpent was cursed to eat dust throughout its life (Gen. 3:14). If humanity is formed from dust, and the serpent is cursed by the Creator God to eat dust, then the mind of humanity is food and a prey to Satan the old serpent. The serpent capitalizes on the naivety and pride of humanity, dominates the reasoning faculty and prompts those who surrender to his craftily and dubious approach to carry out his treacherous will against humanity and the Creator God. If humanity is prey to the serpent then, humanity needs to put off the old self (unguarded dusty mind) and put on the new self (in Christ Jesus).

The merciful God directed Cain's attention to Satan who was behind Cain's deep seated and escalating evil thought and anger against his brother Abel. The treacherous rebel full of sin stood at the door of Cain's first battleground (Cain's thought-life). The deceitful intruder looked for a way to actualize his plan through Cain and falsely vindicate him through his abominable deed (Gen. 4:3-7). Nothing besides Satan (I John 3:8a) inhabited, dominated, led, and prompted Cain to carry out his nefarious and grievous sin of killing Abel (Gen. 4:8). The unfortunate slogan "boredom" did not push Cain to slay Abel, but Satan who worked through the mind of

---

[86] Frangipane, *The Three Battlegrounds*, 11.

Cain by lavishing his evil seed in his mind, and finally consuming his whole soul and body that culminated the first murder case in the Bible and on the earth.

Another battleground of spiritual warfare is the heart. "Keep thy heart with all diligence, for out of it are the issues of life." (Prov. 4:23). When Adam and Eve voluntarily succumbed to Satan's cunning enticement, their hearts were crammed with evil. The battle went on in their hearts (the center of intellect). They doubted God's word in their hearts (Mk. 11:32). Their emotions were aroused by the devil because of their negative anxious hearts (Prov. 12:25). The deceiver then capitalized on their hardened hearts (Ex. 4:21) and craftily persuaded them to actualize their hearts' desire. The totality of their lives swiftly swerved to the brink of embarrassment, bitterness, desperation, insecurity, hopelessness, and separation from their Creator."Let no man say when he is tempted, I am tempted of God: for God cannot be tempted with evil, neither tempted he any man: But every man tempted, when he is drawn away from his own lust, and entices. Then when lust hath conceived, it bringeth forth sin: and sin, when it is finished bringeth forth death." (James 1:13-15). The tempter is aggressively and perpetually inclined to tempt and win humanity through ferocious spiritual battle. God wants to establish His Kingdom in the life of every human being, but the thief strives vigorously through antagonistic schemes to win humanity to his kingdom (the losing side of the spiritual warfare).

"Another frontier of the battle is the heavenly places, the dimension known today as the spirit realm—a place where angels and demons wage war for our cities,"[87] individuals, communities, nations, and geographical regions. "The first heaven is the atmospheric heaven, the sky (Ps.19:1), and the third one is the most familiar definition of heaven: the realms of glory which are crowned by the highest heavens, the dwelling place of God (Matt. 6:9)."[88] If there is a first and a third heaven, then there is a second.

---

[87] Frangipane, *The Three Battlegrounds*, 105.
[88] Ibid., 167.

> The heaven which is the unique object of this study is the spiritual realm which immediately surrounds planet earth and uniquely influences both the consciousness and the sub consciousness of man. It is the realm, known frequently known as the "heavenly places," which is the battleground of our spiritual warfare. Within this realm, good and evil spirits clash in the battle of men's souls.[89]

Unlike the first heaven, which is visible to human eyes, the second heaven is not visible to human eyes. "And there was war in heaven: Michael and his angels fought against the dragon; and the dragon fought and his angels, And prevailed not; neither was their place found any more in heaven, And the great dragon was cast out, that old serpent, called the Devil, and Satan…and his angels were cast out with him" (Rev. 12:7-9). This war occurred in the second heaven—a battlefield or battleground of spiritual warfare. Satan and his angels were displaced (cast out of their comfort zone) by Michael and his loyal angels and took over the spiritual territory ones occupied by Satan and his angels. Woe to the inhabitants of the earth and the sea! For the devil is come down unto you, having great wrath, because he knoweth that he hath but a short time." (Rev. 12:12b) Consumed with outrageous anger, Satan and his fallen angels wage war against most presidents or prime ministers of nations; governors of states and regions; senators; mayors of cities; judges; parliamentarians and other political appointees; and leaders in auxiliary positions. The devil influences them to initiate and implement policies that oppose the precepts of God. Satan and his fallen angels wage war in the heavenly places with the sole purpose of using power-drunk and fame-driven leaders to advocate for and promote nefarious deeds that add more filth and misery to the already depraved situation of humanity. Homosexuality and lesbianism are typical examples of reprehensible deeds initiated by Satan and his fallen angels through some leaders on political and religious platforms.

---

[89] Ibid., 167-168.

THE NATURE OF SPIRITUAL WARFARE

> Homosexuality is categorically prohibited by God in the Old Testament lawsgoverning the sexual life of his people (Lev.18:22; 20:13; Deut. 23:18). It is called "abomination" five times in Leviticus 18 (vv.22, 26, 27, 29, 30). In Leviticus 20:13 it is called "a detestable act." This is consistent with the root meaning of the word which means "to detest," "to hate," or "abhor." It was so detestable a sin in the eyes of God that death by stoning was the punishment inflicted on its practitioners. (Lev. 20:13)[90]

Such leaders advocate through their platforms or portfolios without an iota of indignity to advance the miserable and profane cause of Satan—a recipe for depravity, demoralization, and death.

Edith Honan shares an event about this abnormality:

> (Reuters) – Voters in Maryland, Maine and Washington State approved same-sexmarriage on Tuesday, marking the first time marriage rights have been extended to same sex couple[s] by popular vote. The vote was hailed by [as] a watershed moment by gay rights activists...President Barak Obama this year became the first U.S. president to support gay marriage. His campaign endorsed the gay marriage measures in the three states.[91]

The deceiver—the giver of false hope, the corrupt and evil one—is predisposed to stimulate his captives to engage in detestable things. Satan makes such things very appealing to the carnal mind and the spiritually blind eyes to perpetuate disobedience to God. Consumed with rebellion and pride, Satan roams about with counterfeit promises to those who cling to his wicked words and ways.

---

[90] Murphy, *The Handbook for Spiritual Warfare,"* 137.

[91] Reuters: Maryland, Maine, and Washington State Approve Gay Marriage, http://www.reuters.com/article/2012/11/07/us-usa-campaign-gaymarriage-idUSBRE8A60MG20121107 (Accessed on September 1, 2013).

He lures his allies to reject the truth and accept his sugar-coated and seemingly-good lies. Since antiquity, humanity has been the target of the spiritual battle waged by Satan and his cronies.

"The show of their countenance doth witness against them; and they declare their sin as Sodom, they hide it not. Woe unto their soul! for they have rewarded evil unto themselves" (Isa. 3:9). Activists and advocates of this gross immorality, grievous, and unhealthy sexual relationships placard the excruciating lusts of their hearts. Their hearts (the center of intellect, emotion, and will) are controlled and manipulated by the devil.

The horrible campaign and its deadly outcome is a manifestation of the battle being waged in the heavenly places by Satan and his fallen angels to use world leaders (people of influence) to redefine divine marriage (the first institution by God). In one of their numerous cunning confrontations on pertinent issues, Jesus affirmed the biblical and theological definition of marriage with the following question: "Have you not read, that he which made them at the beginning made them male and female, And said, For this cause shall a man leave father and mother, and they twain shall be one flesh? (Matt. 19:4-5) Then why same-sex marriage? As the enemy took the advantage of the whims and caprice of Eve with lies, so his redefinition of marriage is a blatant lie, insolence, pride, and rebellion against God and God's sovereignty. Even in the animal kingdom, there is nothing like same-sex sexual affairs. Shame on depraved humanity. Pets in the home, animals in the fields, fish in the ocean, and birds in the air are all irrational creatures, but they do not practice same-sex relationships. Why should human beings publicly promote and practice this gross immorality?

"Leaders of NOW, along with feminist activists everywhere, were thrilled to hear the news that the city of San Francisco sanctioned marriage for lesbians and gays, and that Martin 83, and Lyon 79, were the first to marry in an impromptu ceremony."[92] "Activists across the country celebrated as the couple, together for 51 years, became the first same-sex couples to obtain a marriage license and

---

[92] National Organization for Women, Phyllis Lyon and Del Martin Make History Again, (Accessed on September 30, 2013).

marry in United States."⁹³ The two women had lived together as an illegitimate same-sex couple for over 10 decades. After their persistent and brazen argument to support their stand as a lesbian couple, the state of California approved their long fought battle for this detestable marriage which opposes biblical principles of marriage between one man and one woman (Gen. 2:24; Matt. 19:4-5).

In another unfortunate development, Eric Pfeiffer of the Yahoo News reported that "Wisconsin Democratic Rep. Tammy Baldwin was named the projected winner in her race against Republican Tommy Thompson…Baldwin's victory makes her the first openly gay candidate elected to the U.S. Senate."⁹⁴ In an interview with the Guardian, Baldwin said, "We never had an open LGBT member of the U.S. Senate, and even though we strongly advocate pro-equality for those who serve there, it has always been a conversation about a group of people. So this changes everything."⁹⁵ In a message of endorsement and consent, the president of the Gay and Lesbian Alliance Against Defamation (GLAAD) said, "Tammy Baldwin's victory showed a majority of Americans already know: that candidates should be judged on their qualifications on the job and not the sexual orientation."⁹⁶ This is in fulfillment of God's word spoken by Paul, "Professing themselves to be wise, they became fools" (Rom. 1:22). Masquerading themselves to be wiser than the holy God (the initiator of marriage) such people have become miserably confused, morally depraved, and ambiguous in their thinking.

"Laying bare a clash of cultures, President Barak Obama urged African leaders to extend equal rights to gay and lesbians but was bluntly reproved by Senegalese president Macky Sall, who said his country "still isn't ready" to decriminalize homosexuality."⁹⁷ In his

---

⁹³ Ibid.

⁹⁴ Eric Pfeiffer, Yahoo News, "Tammy Baldwin is Elected the First Openly Gay Senator," http://news.yahoo.com/blogs/ticket/tammy-baldwin-elected-first-openly-gay-senator-043558173—election.html (Accessed on November 7, 2013).

⁹⁵Ibid.

⁹⁶Ibid.

⁹⁷ Obama pushes African Leaders on Gay Rights, Rebuked by Senegalese President Macky Sall, http://www.huffingtonpost.com/2013/06/27/obama-africa-gay-rights_n_3512530.html (Accessed on September 2, 2013).

visit to Senegal in West Africa, President Barak Obama tried all he could to persuade his Senegalese counterpart to embrace his campaign for gay marriages and Lesbianism as intense manifestation of the spiritual warfare in the heavenly places. However, in Senegal the forces of Satan in the heavenly places could not persuasively evade the strong moral stand of Senegalese president Macky Sall through his US counterpart to succumb to the evil will of satanic forces. Rather, President Macky Sall who believes that gay marriage is a sinful act punishable by God responded unfavorably to President Obama's sacrilegious proposal.

In his response to the repulsive threats by Prime Minister David Cameron of the United Kingdom to face a slash in British aid if African leaders do not adhere to gay marriages, the late President of Ghana, John Mills, asserted "Ghana's sovereign right to adopt its own laws; and reminded Mr. Cameron that Ghana is no longer under colonial rule, and further reiterated that homosexuality is totally inconsistent with Ghanaian cultural values."[98] I perceive that late President John A. Mills, (a believer in Christ Jesus) responded with the sacred word of the Lord Jesus Christ in his heart. "Man shall not live by bread alone, but by every word that proceedeth out of the mouth of God" (Matt. 4:4).

Though Africa needs aid in many areas, adequate aid without God is worthless and leads to damnation. The battle waged by Satan and his angels in the heavenly places could not fulfill its wanton purpose and mission in the late President John A. Mills of Ghana. In his book titled *Attitude of Gratitude* Dr. Frimpong Manso declares his unwavering support to the late President John Mills of Ghana for unequivocally rejecting the intimidation pressure from the UK Prime Minister David Cameroon for African leaders to succumb to inhuman practices of homosexual marriages in order to receive aid and grants. Dr. Frimpong Manso questions "why someone could come to us and say that until we legally allow our people to practice such a barbaric act as homosexuality, we cannot receive aid from them; what a pity, thank God to this one our president had to say

---

[98] Modern Ghana: President Mills, Prime Minister Cameron on Homosexual Rights, http://www.modernghana.com/news/359362/1/president-mills-prime-minister-cameron-and-homosex.html (Accessed on September 1, 2013).

no."[99] The world needs political leaders like President Macky Sall of Senegal and late President John Mills of Ghana to champion the cause of the Kingdom of God by thwarting the works of the devil through leaders who are being influenced by "the prince and power of the air, the spirit that now worketh in the children of the disobedience." (Eph. 2:2b).

In another Satan-motivated development to use world leaders to redefine marriage and sexual relationship through Mr. Cameron's repugnant ambition campaigning in favor of homosexual activities Nigerians have condemned the reported plan by the Prime Minister, Mr. David Cameron to embark on a campaign to globalize gay marriage, saying that there is no room for such alien culture in Nigeria. "Cameron said he would deploy his ministers to different parts of the world to carry the campaign. According to Mr. Cameron, the best place to be gay, lesbian and transgender is anywhere in Europe."[100] Unlike Africa that has majority of its countries categorized among developing or third world countries, almost all the countries in Europe are in the developed countries status. However, one of the strange issues is that Mr. Cameron advocates that gay, lesbian, and transgender activists are welcome in Europe—a safe haven for such unfortunate and licentious sexual relationships.

Still on this primitive act of moral indecency "Australia's Prime Minister, Mr. Kevin Rudd has pledged to legalize gay marriage within 100 days of office, should he win the election on September 7, calling the measure a "mark of decency". He opposed gay marriage during his first term as prime minister he changed his mind after discussions with people including his daughter Jessica."[101] Is this change of mind and heart's desire of Australia's Prime Minister Kevin Rudd positive in the eyes of God or the populace? It is bogus

---

[99] Paul Frimpong Manso, *Attitude of Gratitude"* (Accra: Tent Media Publication, 2011), 35.

[100] Nigeria: British PM Vows to Export Gay Marriage Nationwide, http://leadership.ng/news/260713/british-pm-vows-export-gay-marriage-worldwide (Accessed on August 29, 2013).

[101] The Huffington Post United Kingdom: Australia's Prime Minister Kevin Rudd Pledges to Introduce Gay Marriage, http://www.huffingtonpost.com/2013/08/13/kevin-rudd-australia-gay-marriage-_n_3741655.html (Accessed on September 2, 2013).

and bigotry in the Kingdom of Light and Life but very welcome and pleasing in the kingdom of darkness doom, and destruction.

Why this huge turning from "grace to grass"? The spiritual warfare escalates daily because the enemy is furious to destroy humanity, and moreover, majority of people with "big platforms" and "big microphones" easily fall prey to the wicked plans of Satan to intensify his warfare against the marvelous plan of God for humanity. The enemy wins the whims and caprices of his captors and lavish his characters like; power hunger, vain glory, egocentricity, pride, hypocrisy and deceitfulness. The initiator of spiritual warfare (Satan), also known as the deceiver, the lair and the father of all lies, the intruder, the murderer, the serpent, the tempter is behind such acts of gross impertinence of such leaders against God.

The last battlefield in this book is "the Church." After Jesus cast a devil out of a dumb person, some accused Him of casting out demons through Beelzebub the chief of devils (Luke 11:14-15). In response to their naïve and unfounded accusations Jesus proved to them that He did not cast out devils through Beelzebub:"Every kingdom divided against itself is brought to desolation: and a house divided against a house falleth" (Luke 11:17). Thus, Satan cannot cast out satanic spirits.

Frangipane's ecclesiological approach in this context is noteworthy;

> The other born-again congregations in our cities are not our enemies! We must learn to war against the illusions and strife, the fears and jealousies that are sent from hell to divide us. If Jesus is eternally praying for our oneness (John 17:20-23 then we must recognize that Satan is continually fighting against it. The devil knows that when we become one with Christ and, through Him, one with each other, it is only a matter of time before this Jesus-built church will destroy the empire of hell![102]

---

[102] Francis Frangipane, *The Three Battlegrounds*, 61.

Born again (John 3: 3) believers are those that are born of the Spirit (John 3:5-6) by accepting Jesus Christ as personal Lord and Savior and are led by the Spirit of God (Rom. 8:14). They are the Church, one of the battlegrounds of Satan and his evil forces. The Lord of the Church prays and expects that His church would be a piercing dynamic force against the wiles and weapons of satanic forces, but unfortunately various congregations demonstrate frictions and hostilities in myriads of ways initiated and wrought by Satan to prevail over the Church. Sneaky Satan knows the power and authority in Spirit-led, Spirit-motivated, and Spirit-backed unity. Crafty Satan diverts the attention of the Church from coming together as a formidable force to work alongside the Spirit of God to build the Church of Jesus Christ. Rather, antagonist Satan lavishes his deadly characters upon the church for effective use against the community of faith in Jesus. Thus, unfortunately, the church wages war against itself. Therefore, the Church is inadequately fighting the good fight of faith against the common enemy. Any kingdom that fights against itself disseminates.

Satan and his fallen angels wage war against "the Church" of Jesus Christ. I don't mean "the Church of Jesus Christ of Latter Day Saints." Then, what is "the Church"? The Church is called "the people of God", "the Messianic Community", "the Body of Christ", and "the fellowship of the Spirit".[103] "The English word "church" derives from the late Greek word *kyriakon,* the Lord's house, a church building, and in the NT the word translates the Greek word *ekklesia.*"[104]

A concise definition by Clowney helps in this discussion:

> The church may be defined as God sees it the so-called "church invisible". This is composed of all whose names are in the Lamb's book of life (Rev. 21:27). The "church visible," on the other hand, is the church as we see it, the family of believers. The

---

[103] E. P. Clowney, "Church," in *New Dictionary of Theology,* ed. Sinclair B. Ferguson, (Downers Grove: InterVarsity Press, 1988), 140-141.

[104] Roger. L. Omanson, "The Church," in *Evangelical Dictionary of Theology,* ed. Walter Elwell, (Grand Rapids: Baker Books, 1999), 231.

distinction guards against equating membership in the church visible with salvation, or, on the other hand, disregarding public identification with God's people.[105]

The thoughts of God are not the thoughts of humanity, neither His ways ours (Isa. 55:8). Then, the way God interprets and comprehends things is not the way humanity does. Though the Church is comprised of all who profess Jesus Christ as Lord and Savior, there is a significant dichotomy between the "Church invisible" and the "Church visible." It is only the Lord of the Church who knows the "invisible Church" for He "knoweth them that are his" (2 Tim. 2:19). The Omniscient God knows the faithful ones among the "visible Church." The Lord of the Church says, "Not everyone that saith unto me, Lord, Lord, shall enter into the kingdom of heaven; but he that doeth the will of my Father which is in heaven" (Matt. 7:21) — the redeemed ones that are bought by the Blood of the Lamb, committed to the cause of God, and eagerly waiting for the coming of the Glorious Lord and Savior Jesus Christ.

"The Church may also be viewed as an *organism* in which every member functions and associates with other members, and also as an *organization* in which are exercised the various gifts of the Spirit."[106] As an organization, members of a particular temple or church building or even in a particular religious organization, are viewed and classified as members of the "visible Church." "Throughout history the nature of the church has been defined by divided Christians trying to establish the validity of their own existence."[107] This is an avenue by which the arch enemy of Jesus and His Church wages persistent war in the Church. He uses division and dissention, resentment and rivalry, self abasement and self-sufficient, and self- righteous and self-aggrandizement. Few examples are;

---

[105] Clowney, "Church," 141.

[106] Clowney, "Church," 141.

[107] Omanson, "The Church," 231.

The Donatists of North Africa in the early centuries focused on the purity of the church and claimed to be the only church that measured up to the biblical standard. In the Middle Ages various sects defines the church in as to claim that they, and not the Roman Catholic Church, were the true church. The Arnoldistem emphasized poverty and identification with the masses; the Waldenses stressed literal obedience to Jesus' teachings and emphasized evangelical preaching. Roman Catholics claim that the only true church was that over which the pope was supreme as the successor of the apostle Peter.[108]

With the ascendancy of various doctrines and theologies, the tendency to strive and secede invite disunity, division, and "internal warfare"—fighting within the Church instead of "external warfare"—jointly fighting against the common enemy Satan and his evil forces. This makes the Church a battlefield of spiritual warfare. Nonetheless, the Lord Jesus Christ prays and anticipates that His Church will be a sacred united force, impenetrable and unbreakable despite the evil intentions of Satan and the gates of hell (John 17:20-21; Matt. 16:18).

The Weapons of Spiritual Warfare

Webster defines weapon as "something (as a club, knife or gun) used to injure, defeat, or destroy."[109] It is biblically sound that "God is a Spirit." (John 4:24). Satan the arch enemy and his fallen angels are spiritual creatures. Therefore, I vehemently support the biblical and theological prudence that the weapons of spiritual warfare are not physical weapons like guns, axes, knives, cutlasses bows and arrows that are sold in shops, stores, and malls, but spiritual weapons are spiritual (2 Cor. 10:3-5).

---

[108] Ibid.

[109] Merriam-Webster, *Merriam-Webster's Collegiate Dictionary, Eleventh Edition* (Springfield: Merriam-Webster Incorporated, 2005), 1417.

Dr. Evans shares the following insights on this subject:

> Satan's attacks come from the unseen realm of the spirit. So if you don't use God's spiritual weapon to fight your spiritual battle, you are going to war with a cap pistol. An example of a cap pistol is "anger." But anger is a human weapon that does not work against a spiritual enemy. You can't use human weapons to win spiritual war. The devil is too crafty for us. He has schemes and plans we can't even see. We need the armor of God because of the war we are up against.[110]

Some examples of carnal weapons that Satan prompts unbelieving hearts to use are; characters, natural abilities and achievements like anger, aggression, pride, stature, color, beauty, wealth, power of positive thinking, lusts, and many more. Human weapons are inappropriate, and very inferior to counterattack and subdue satanic forces and weapons. Satan blindfolds the spiritual eyes and minds of humanity and deprives many from comprehending the biblical and theological understanding of spiritual warfare and its spiritual weapons.

Ignorance of God and His Word creates a huge avenue for the intruder to freely dominate the minds and the hearts of such captors of the devil. After making his abode in their lives through dubious enticements he further misinterprets to them that there is nothing like Satan. Sadly enough, the devil imprints in the minds and hearts of his subjects of his non-existence. At that peak of insensitivity to the things of the Kingdom of God he uses his subjects to defend his wicked deeds against themselves and others. The enemy feels very comfortable when the same people (his agents) he is destroying cover him up about his evil deeds.

If the spiritual warfare is waged in the spiritual realm, then what are the spiritual weapons of the warfare used by Satan? Ignorance of the weapons of the arch enemy is fatal lose on the part of whoever

---

[110] Evans, *The Battle is of the Lord's*, 262.

counterattacks him. In dealing with satanic weapons, sin, the flesh, and the world are the premise on which he battles against humanity.

What is sin? Colwell's elaboration of sin helps in this discussion:

> Scripture employs a variety of words to speak of sin, with meanings ranging from "the missing of a mark or goal" or "the breach of relationship to "ungodliness", "perversion" or "rebellion". Yet the common theme of every biblical expression of the nature of sin is the central idea that sin is a state of our being that separates us from the holy God; biblically, sin is ultimately sin against God.[111]

All the above various terms tantamount to disobedience to God, violation of God's will, or rebellion against God's cause. Augustine defines the essence of sin as concupiscence *(concupiscentia),* as the perverted self-love which is the opposite of love for God.[112] Jesus mentions that Satan began to sin (I John 3:8), thus the originator and initiator of sin through lies to fallen angels and humanity, and pride and rebellion toward God—the primary cause of separation of both angels and humanity from God unto condemnation. (Jer. 31:30).

"Now the works of the flesh are manifest, which are these; adultery, fornication, uncleanness, lasciviousness, Idolatry, witchcraft, hatred, variance, emulations, wrath, strife, seditions, and heresies. Envyings, murders, drunkenness, revelings, and such like:..they that which do such things shall not inherit the kingdom of God" (Gal. 5:19-21). When humanity succumbs to the works of the flesh through diverse enticements of the devil and subsequently actualize them, then the outcome becomes sin against God. (James 4:4). God forewarned Cain that "...sin lieth at the door. And unto thee shall be his desire, and thou shalt rule over him." (Gen. 4:7b). However, Cain beckoned to the lust of his treacherous master "the father of all lies", "the murderer", "the devil", and he sinned against God by murdering his brother. (Gen. 4:8). The devil monopolized Cain's

---

[111] J. E. Colwell, "Sin," in *New Dictionary of Theology*, ed. Sinclair Ferguson (Downers Grove: InterVarsity Press, 1988), 641.

[112] Ibid., 641-642.

fleshy lust and desire that prematurely broke his (Cain) relationship with God—eternal separation from God.

"The world" is one of the avenues that the arch enemy of God and humanity uses as weapon for spiritual warfare against humanity. But there is more than one interpretation of the word "world".

Barclay provides a concise understanding of the two views of the world: In a few biblical passages the word "world" (kosmos) is used in the sense of

> mankind. In John 3:16, for instance, we are told of God's love for" the world" in this sense. When this is what is meant, then the Christian duty to love mankind is clear. It is in the other, and more usual, that there are more problems. In this wider sense "the world" usually means "the environment of humanity". That is to say, it includes not only the natural environment and all its varied resources, but also the cultural and social environment brought into being by sinful humanity. In this sense, the devil is described as the "prince" or "ruler of this world" who was condemned and cast out by the power and work of Christ (John 12:31; 16:11; Eph. 6:12).[113]

In this context, I am focusing on "the environment of humanity." The enemy uses detestable cultures, traditions, societal norms, dress codes, music, films and movies, video games among others and even manipulates through science and technology, academic pursuit, and heretical philosophies as weapons of spiritual warfare against humanity. Scripture strongly advocates that; association or alignment with "the world" is hostility, disrespect, automatic disassociation with God (James 4:4).

The greatest weapon the enemy uses is lies (Gen. 3:1-5; John 8:44). With this biblical truth in mind, I unequivocally agree with Frangipane's argument that;

---

[113] O. R. Barclay, "World" in *New Dictionary of Theology* ed. Sinclair Ferguson (Downers Grove: InterVarsity Press, 1988), 729.

> The most irrevocable and spiritually sophisticated weapon God has given us (the redeemed in Christ) to combat the death trapped-lies of the enemy (Satan) is the Word of God, which the Scriptures refer to as the "sword of the Spirit" (Ephesians. 6:17). Jesus Christ said His words "are spirit and are life" (John 6:63), which is to say that the substance or meaning in Christ's words represents an actual reality: the living Spirit of the Kingdom of God. [114]

The Lord of the Church, Jesus Christ, used the Word of God in His counter-action to Satan's misleading and out-of-context quotes for tempting Jesus Christ (Luke. 4:1-13). The phrase "it is written," appears twice (Luke 4:4; 8), and "it is said," appears once (Luke 4:12) If "the disciple is not above his master, nor the servant above his lord" (Matt. 10:24), and the Master used the Word of God then, there is no excuse for disciples of the Master (subjects of the kingdom of God) to deny the appropriateness and efficacy of the Word of God as the number one weapon of spiritual warfare against the arch enemy. The tendency or temptation for Disciples of Christ to ignore or underestimate this biblical and theological concept in defense and subsequent triumph in spiritual warfare with the devil, inevitably leads to devastation and defeat of subjects of the Kingdom of God. There are few pertinent points that I recognize as appropriate to support my argument that the Word of God is the divinely foundational weapon to victoriously battle against satanic forces and agents.

1. Though the devil may misquote Scripture as in the case of his thorough humiliation and outstanding defeat by Christ in the wilderness (Matt. 4:1-11), right application of the Word of God through diligent studies in the leading of the Holy Spirit perpetuates Christ victory over Satan on behalf of the believer in Christ.

---

[114] Francis Frangipane, *The Three Battlegrounds*, 111.

2. All textbooks, journals, Guinness Record Book, Treasury Bills, Constitutions of nations and businesses, and other religious literature among others are human made with myriads of amendments, flaws, and biases. Besides fictitious amendments, these documents do not have divine authority and inerrancy as does the Word of God. God is the author of the Word of God (Ps. 119:89; Isa. 40:8; Mk. 13:31; 2 Tim. 3:16).
3. With reverential fear and absolute recognition to the Word of God, the Psalmist says, "Thy word is a lamp unto my feet, and a light unto my path" (Ps. 119:105). Literally, lamp is warmth, it draws creatures both rational and irrational, drives out darkness, and serves as the epitome of a compass in one's daily walk. As light, God's word is a life sustaining vehicle for a child of God's victorious life journey. This occurs even in the midst of escalating spiritual warfare with satanic forces and satanic agents. Also, "The entrance of thy words giveth light, it giveth understanding unto the simple" (Ps. 119:130). Earthly wisdom is from the devil, but heavenly wisdom is from God (James 3:13-17). The power in the Word of God conveys a supernatural light that dispels the power of darkness and its skeptical view of the things of God. By prevailing over the carnal mind, the Word of God enables humble recipients to gain theological and biblical insight and comprehension into God's wisdom and revelation.

The previously foolish, disobedient, and skeptical author of this book gained understanding about twenty-one years ago after the Word of God had been taught and preached to him in the power and prudence of the Holy Spirit. God's Word never returns to him void (Isa. 55:11). Whenever the Word of God is shared, preached, or taught in the leading and power of the Spirit of God it breaks the concrete of hostility and enmity, dispels and disapproves the powers and works of darkness, frees captives from the domain of the devil, opens the spiritual mind and eyes of captives, and motivates humble adherents to surrender to the exclusive lordship of Christ Jesus. The enemy blindfolds human beings from seeing and coming to glorious God through His Son Jesus Christ; however, the Holy Spirit uses the Word of God to open the eyes of the spiritually blind and carnally minded skeptic, reveals a glimpse of the truth, and consumes the carnal mind with reverential fear of the living God for a lifelong adventure with Christ.

Islam believes and teaches that their holy book *Qur'an* was given to Muhammad by the archangel Gabriel[115] but the inspired and inerrant sacred literature that repudiates and nullifies the aforementioned false belief and teaching of Islam is the Word of God—the Christian Holy Bible. The Word of God declares that God spoke through a variety of ways and different servants of His inspired by His Spirit in different times, but lastly He speaks through His only Son Jesus Christ (Heb. 1:1-3). Thus, "Jesus inaugurated a new age altogether— the Messianic Age,"[116] a fulfillment of what the prophets said about the Son of God (Isa. 7:14; 9:6-7; Matt. 1:21-23). "As a prophet (Luke 24:19), priest (Heb. 7:3), and king (Rev. 17:14). Jesus is more than simply the last in the line of prophets,"[117] and more than an ordinary prophet. As One of the Triune God (Matt. 28:19) Jesus and the Father are One (John 10:30; 14:9). Islam's prophet Mohammad leads so many people to damnation through his false and heretical teachings (John 3:36), but Jesus is the way to the Father (John 14:6). After His atoning death and His glorious resurrection on behalf of wayward humanity (Rom. 4:25), Jesus Christ ascended back to heaven, and will come back to earth according to the Word of God (Acts 1:11).

Waging Spiritual Warfare

"Stand up, stand up for Jesus, ye soldiers of the Cross, Lift his high His royal banner, it must not suffer loss, from victory unto victory, His army shall He lead till every foe is vanquished, and Christ is Lord indeed."[118] Spiritual warfare is waged according to biblical principles. Victory in the warfare is appropriated in the way

---

[115] Warren Matthews, *World Religions: Sixth Edition* (Belmont: Wadsworth Gengage Learning, 2007), 326.

[116] Kenneth Baker and John Kohlenberger III, *Zondervan NIV Bible Commentary Vol. 2. New Testament* (Grand Rapids: Zondervan Publishing House, 1994), 943.

[117] Ibid., 943.

[118] *Hymns of Glorious Praise*, (Springfield: Gospel Publishing House, 1969), 412.

the Champion Jesus Christ deems it fitting. The enemy and his allies would be destroyed on the sole condition of engaging spiritual warfare with divine weapons and approach to combat Satanic powers and lift the victorious banner of Jesus Christ high above all kingdoms, authorities, and dominions.

"No man that warreth entangleth himself with the affairs of this life; that he may please him who hath chosen him to be a soldier. And if a man also strive for masteries, yet is he not crowned, except he strive lawfully" (2 Tim. 2:4-5). In his epistle to Timothy, the apostle Paul circumspectly likened him to the physical or human soldier on the battlefield fighting a physical battle. The physical or human solider should war according to the law of earthly or human warfare in order to please his or her captain and finally emerge victorious. Soldiers of the Cross of the risen Jesus Christ—children or subjects of the Kingdom of God are strictly obliged by the King of the Kingdom to fight the good fight of faith spiritually on the firm premise of fervent faith in Jesus Christ and doing warfare according to His teachings.

"The warfare between the power of the devil and power of God in the life of believers"[119] in Christ Jesus is waged in biblical and theological perspectives. A vivid illustration of waging spiritual warfare is in the Christian Bible (Eph. 6:10-13).

Believers in Christ Jesus or subjects of the kingdom of God are persistently cautioned to be discerning and humble, and to maintain a mindset of emptiness without the ability and capability of the all-sufficient God. Believers in Christ are not to trust in their own fragile and vulnerable strength, as compared to the devil's craftiness and enticements. Though it is unscriptural to exaggerate the reality, existence, and deadly weapons of Satan and his allies against humanity and the Church of Jesus Christ, it is equally unscriptural for believers in Christ to deny Satan's wicked intentions or underestimate his destructive expectation for humanity.

"Scripture authenticates the reality of the spirit world, including angelic friends and demonic foes."[120] Demonic foes are led by Satan

---

[119] Murphy, 402.

[120] Ibid.," 88.

THE NATURE OF SPIRITUAL WARFARE

in rebellion against God and His loyal angels (Rev. 12:7-9). After suffering a great defeat at the hands of Michael the archangel of God Satan and his allied demons were cast out from the heaven with fierce anger against the inhabitants of the earth—the habitation of humanity. With the biblical perspective of the reality and existence of demonic foes with their leader the prince of the power of the air (Eph. 2:2), it is very prudent to learn and understand how to wage spiritual warfare against the opposing powers and appropriate the victory of Jesus Christ. Without an iota of doubt the generous God has provided whatever is needful for subjects of the Kingdom of God to be "overcoming Christian soldiers"—more than conqueror (Rom. 8:37) soldiers of the Cross, but victory is appropriated with genuine recognition and reverence to Jesus Christ and His Word.

""Finally" is followed immediately by three imperatives,"[121] be strong in the Lord (Eph. 6: 10); put on the whole armor of God (Eph. 6:11); and take unto you the whole armor of God (Eph. 6:13). This means in order to counterattack, resist, and defeat the archenemy there is absolute significant need of the strength and power of the One who is greater than the devil—the Omnipotent God. That old serpent, called the devil, and Satan (Rev. 12:9) is crafty, cunning, and stronger than humanity without the divine power. The warfare is not against fellow human beings, beasts, and inanimate objects. Rather, it is against unseen powers the Christian Holy Bible talks about. Hence to wage effective spiritual warfare is to hit the target—satanic powers, but not to hit off target—humanity. To experience Christ' outstanding victory over demonic forces, I counsel children of the Kingdom of God to go to the offensive and counter attack the power of darkness with the full armor of God according to the biblical truth.

Lowenberg's advice helps in this discussion;

> When necessary, Christians should be confident to engage in power encounters. They should emulate Jesus when, by the Spirit, He confronted Satan. He overcame the devil's temptation by declaring

---
[121] Murphy, 403.

the truths of God's Word, safeguarding His relation with the Father through obedience and by remaining humble and dependent on God's provisions, timing, and ways. Jesus has given power and authority to His disciples to drive out demons, heal sicknesses and diseases, and preach the kingdom of God (Mark 16:15-18; Luke 9:1, 2).[122]

Jesus Christ humiliated and thwarted Satan and his evil initiative in the wilderness by speaking the Word of God (Luke 4:1-13). Proclamation, speaking, teaching, or preaching the Word of God should not be overlooked or underestimated in the believer's warfare with the opposing powers and authorities. If the Master Himself spoke the powerful Word of God to counteract the devils subtlety, then His servants (subjects of the Kingdom of God) are obliged to follow His examples to appropriate His victory over all assailing authorities and powers. Demons tremble and flee out of their captors (Acts 16:16-18) and various healings are experienced by the afflicted and the sick (Acts 3:1-10) at the preaching of the Kingdom of God. With the mandated power and authority given by the Master to His disciples or believers in Him, the Kingdom of God advances through aggressive encounters with wicked and evil spirits by the power and authority of the non-negotiable Word of God in the ongoing spiritual warfare.

In his inspiring book titled, *10 Amazing Muslims Touched by God,* Guclu (Corey) Erman narrates his encounter with Christ that compelled him to preach the kingdom of God with unprecedented results;

> What happened to them happened to me—the infilling of the Holy Spirit with evidence of speaking in other tongues (see Acts 2:4; Matt. 3:11; Luke 3:16)...A few days later I prayed for a Muslim girl with a golf-sized tumor on her neck. The minute I

---

[122] Doug Lowenberg, "Spiritual Warfare, Demonization and the Christian Life: How the Devil Influences Believers," *Enriching, and Equipping Spirit-Filled Ministers,* Vol. 18, no 3 (June 2013) 94-95.

> touched her she screamed out saying my hand burned her—she felt the fire of God—and the tumor entirely disappeared! It's been like that ever since on hundred occasions. As I write this, it has been 14 years that I have dedicated my life full-time to ministry in Turkey, preaching the Gospel to the Muslims as God confirms His Word with signs and wonders and miracles and brings many into the assurance of His love, now and forever.[123]

Spirit anointed preaching and teaching the Word of God always give birth to supernatural harvest of souls. Harvest of souls come after satanic forces are subdued, blindfolded, relinquished of their spoils, and their captives delivered by the matchless power and authority of God and His Word. Then, former captives of the prince of the air (Eph. 2:2) are taken away from captivity and domain of the deceiver and they declare their solemn allegiance, reverence, and recognition to the Son of God as their personal Lord and Savior. Healings and other miracles apart from the topmost miracle of salvation are by products or bonuses to compliment God's Word. God's Word is a consuming fire (Jer. 5:14) that annihilates opposing powers, their demonic shackles, diverse impediments, and myriads of inflicted afflictions.

Biblical truth is irrevocable, biblical truth is God Word, biblical truth is life and living, biblical truth is power encounter against the defeated foe—"the adversarial spirit, who acts as the tempter and accuser and who is an enemy of the work of God in creation and human affairs.[124] As the father of all liars (John 8:44)), the enemy of God and humanity cannot prevail over Biblical truth.

In his theological counsel to the saints in Ephesus on the subject of waging spiritual warfare the apostle Paul uses metaphors to describe and reveal the approach to victorious combat against the archenemy and his allied agents. "Stand therefore, having your loins

---

[123] Faisal Malick, *10 Amazing Muslims Touched By God,* (Carol Stream: Tyndale House Publishers Inc., 2012), 90.

[124] Louisiana Baptist University, Statement of Faith, http://lbu.edu/statement%20of%20faith.html (Accessed on September 18, 2013).

girt about with truth," (Eph. 6:14a). In this context, ""the truth" is the word of truth, that is, the Gospel and Jesus as the truth; the truth is the absence of all deceit."[125] Lowenberg posits that "clinched around the center of one's being must be truthfulness, honesty, and integrity."[126] Biblical truth is a weapon that wards off the outrageous move of the devil. Hence, there is a significant need for believers in Christ or subjects of the kingdom of God to remain trustworthy in the eyes of God.

The devil manipulates on the fragility of human affections (Gen. 3; Gal. 5:19-21). Human affections can be protected and preserved by constantly putting on the "breastplate of righteousness" (Eph. 6:14b) in God's perspective—righteousness that comes from faith in Jesus Christ. Hitherto, the believer is also cautioned to live a righteous life. Righteous living is a dominant force against the wiles of the enemy. The enemy is a liar and can neither stand against the righteousness of God, nor can he penetrate the breastplate of righteousness into the heart of the believer in Christ to dominate, destroy, and kill.

"And your feet shod with the preparation of the gospel of peace" (Eph.6:15). A serious and devoted athlete never wears heel to compete with opponents for a crown. Appropriate sports shoe is fitting and easy to run with when the whistle is blown for commencement of a race or a game. In like manner the required metaphoric shoe for the spiritual soldier or athlete in spiritual warfare is the gospel of peace—to run with the fragrance of peace to wherever the Master sends into the dying world to evoke the peace of God that surpasses all understanding. Even in the midst of chaos, war, tragedy, and other emotional, mental, psychological trauma the soldier of the Cross should be ready for spiritual combat with the Gospel of peace against the arch enemy. Firm footing on the "Solid Rock" demonstrates readiness and preparedness to proceed to subdue spiritual hurricanes and other devilish forces that fight against the cause of God. The gospel of peace is a divine weapon that subdues restlessness and other afflictions of the enemy (Matt. 11:28).

---

[125] Murphy, 409.

[126] Lowenberg, 95.

"Above all, taking the shield of faith, wherewith ye shall be able to quench all the fiery darts of the wicked" (Eph.6:16). Holding sternly to the biblical promises allows the believer to ward off and suffocate the deadly attempts of the devil[127] to traumatize and paralyze the faith of the believer and his subsequent doom and destruction. Faith is a powerful weapon with which the believer in Christ puts the devourer to flight whenever he charges against the cause of God. Faithlessness is a serious sin (Heb. 11:6), and it is one of the fiercest weapons Satan uses in spiritual warfare. The believer's adoption into the family of God, and his or her walk and work with Christ Jesus to fulfill God's calling is by faith. Through diverse forms of intimidation and fear, the enemy infuses doubt, skepticism, unbelief, and faithlessness in the life of the believer in Christ. Then, how can faith be activated and grow? "… faith cometh by hearing, and hearing by the word of God" (Rom. 10:17). While the enemy feeds the affections of the believer with fear and other negativities to steal and disengage his target (the child of God), constant feeding, meditating, pondering, and incarnating the Word of God accentuates the faith of the believer to stand tall, step into the unknown, counter-confront satanic powers and authorities, and paralyzes the wicked zeal and anticipations of the evil one.

"A warrior who never attacks the enemy, but only defends himself, is a trapped warrior;"[128] and the propensity of being defeated is predictable. Equating this to the boxer in the ring with his opponent, the one who gets stuck at the corner receives merciless and brutal punches or blows from his opponent. There should always be a balance—both defensive and offensive. After metaphorically talking about the defensive weapons (above), Paul adds the offensive weapon to balance the approach to wage victorious spiritual warfare. "And take the helmet of salvation, and the sword of the Spirit, which is the word of God." (Eph. 6:17). "The helmet of salvation protects us from the most fatal of all blows to a child of God, the doubts about his acceptance 'warts and all' by God."[129] With the

---

[127] Lowenberg, 95.

[128] Murphy, 408.

[129] Ibid., 411.

assurance of salvation, children of God are very optimistic of the outcome of spiritual warfare—thus, the helmet of salvation on the head of the believer in Christ. Therefore, Paul implores a soldier of the Cross (subject of the kingdom of God) to wage spiritual warfare with that bounding and unwavering awareness of active faith in the Rock of our salvation (Ps. 95:1) with biblically sound and theologically defensive and offensive strategies (diverse pieces of armor coming together as the whole armor of God).

The sword of the Spirit is the spiritual soldier's offensive weapon used in waging spiritual warfare against satanic agents and forces. The deceiver pollutes the minds of humanity, especially some scientists, to view the Christian Holy Bible as a myth or man-made book. In her book titled *Why I Believe the Bible is the Word of God* Phyllis Robinson "says scientific evidence of God is now increasing rapidly—and gradually the scientific world is becoming aware of many new breakthroughs."[130] I unfold few examples on this subject in the following paragraphs.

A scholar and former atheist Patrick Glynn, explains in *God: The Evidence,* that modern thinkers assumed science would reveal the universe to be ever more random and mechanical; instead it has discovered unexpected new layers of intricate order that bespeak an almost unimaginably vast master design.[131] Interestingly enough, the glorious light of the sword of the Spirit (the Word of God) diminishes the dark cloud of the deceived mind and perverted heart, illuminates the reasoning faculty of the most skeptic person, and finally brings creates the awareness of one's conversion, call, commission, and command with the same Word of God he frowned at.

As "the liar and the father of all liars" (John 8:44), the enemy tries his best to craftily convince humanity to disbelieve the flawlessness, authenticity, and sacredness of the sword of the Spirit. He approached Adam and Eve in the Garden of Eden and succeeded in his malice and deceitfulness (Gen. 3). However, the more Satan attempts to discredit and subject the Word of God to disrepute, the more the Spirit of God opens the minds of skeptics and atheists to

---

[130] Phyllis Robinson, *Why I Believe the Bible is the Word of God* (Tennessee: Thomas Nelson Inc., 2012), 36-37.

[131] Ibid., 37.

embrace it while further drawing them into a perpetual adventure with the Son of God through exclusive faith in Him. In support of this argument, Robinson prudently asserts her claims in this way:

> Morrison was a lawyer who wanted to write a book against the resurrection of Jesus Christ. His first chapter was entitled "The Book That Refused to Be Written" because in his research in preparation for writing, he found the evidence so overwhelming that he became a believer...Morrison gives us some interesting food for thought. Thus, the Romans were interested in keeping the province quite. Stealing the body of Jesus would not have benefited them. The Jews, in general, did not believe this humble Nazarene was their Messiah and asked that the believers could not steal the body. The third group, the disciples certainly had no reason to steal the body. So, who was left to steal the body of Jesus?[132]

No amount of lies can deny the truth. Rather, Morrison's quest to repudiate and humiliate the authenticity of the sword of the Spirit in regards to the resurrection of Jesus Christ had an adverse effect on his life. Highly sophisticated weaponry it is, "the Word of God, which is the sword of the Spirit" (Eph. 6:17) dominated Morrison's carnal mind and his negative approach and rather, enlightened him, gave him clear understanding of the truth, and finally drew him from the kingdom of doom and destruction into the glorious Kingdom of Light and Life through faith in Christ Jesus. Interestingly, the sword of the Spirit that was once offensive to Morrison later became his offensive weapon to defend the biblical truth by denying the hollow and baseless lies of Satan. The Christian Holy Bible, "The sword of the Spirit, which is the word of God" (Eph. 6:17) is the target of the enemy to annihilate it from the surface of the earth.

In antiquity king Jehoiakim of Judah was influenced and initiated aggressively by the arch enemy to burn part of the prophetic

---

[132] Robinson, 86-88.

word of God spoken through the prophet Jeremiah. "The word of the LORD came to Jeremiah, after that the king had burned the roll, and the words which Baruch wrote at the mouth of Jeremiah saying, Take thee again another roll, and write in it all the former words that were in the first roll, which Jehoiakim the king of Judah hath burned" (Jer. 36:27-28). Unfortunately for king Jehoiakim of Judah, the Omnipotent God penned the same words through His prophet Jeremiah. "So Jeremiah took another scroll and gave it to the scribe Baruch son of Neriah, and as Jeremiah dictated, Baruch wrote on it all the words of the scroll that Jehoiakim king of Judah had burned in the fire...Many similar words were added to them"(Jer. 36:32). Besides re-writing the spoken words that was burned by Jehoikim, God pronounced inescapable judgment to rebellious king Jehoiakim of Judah through Jeremiah the prophet (Jer. 36:29b-31).

In another development Ingersoll's attitude, pronouncement, and expectation against, "the Word of God, which is the sword of the Spirit" (Eph. 6:17) was turned by God in a way that gives glory to Him alone and serves as a catalyst of nourishment to soldiers of the Cross. God's mighty opposing move against Ingersoll's ultimate rebellious and insolent attitude to God and His Word, blatantly denies all lies, profanity, irreverence, and ugly approaches to the sacredness of the Holy Bible as a firm base to wage victorious spiritual warfare.

Robinson unfolds the death and humiliation of Ingersoll:

> Throughout history people have sought to eradicate the witness of Christians. In A.D.303 an edict was issued to destroy all of the world's Bibles. People found with Bibles were killed. In Nazi Germany people used to hide their Bibles in their floor bins. The agnostic, Ingersoll, held up a copy of the Bible and said, "In fifteen years I'll have this book in the morgue." Fifteen years rolled by, Ingersoll was in the morgue, and the Bible lived on.[133]

---

[133] Robinson, 89.

Jesus says, "Heaven and earth shall pass away; but my words shall not pass away" (Mark 13:31). Ingersoll's legacy of gross rebellion and fatally humiliating agnosticism is a great lesson for all who may be like minded, not to attempt to fight against "the two-edged sword" (Heb. 4:12). The wrath of God and His Word transcends ages. Attacking the Word of God is fighting a losing battle against the Spirit of God because the infallible Word is God-breathed (2 Tim. 3:16).

"The Word of God" is a dynamic weapon to wage war against the lies, wiles, and weapons of Satan and his allies.

Again, Phyllis Robinson says;

> Voltaire said that in one hundred years the Bible would be an outmoded and forgotten book, to be found only in museums. When the one hundred years were up; Voltaire's house was owned and used by the Geneva Bible Society. And recently, ninety-two volumes of Voltaire's works were sold for two dollars (E. M. Harrison). God's Word lives on as a testimony of the resurrected Christ.[134]

If Voltaire can come back from his grave alive and have a glimpse of his own house now owned and populated with Bibles and other Biblical literature of Geneva Bible Society, what would be his reaction? Would he disallow or allow his home to be used for the very purpose he falsely, ignorantly, and arrogantly predicted against? The Author of life took away Voltaire's life, but the Word of God is unabatedly the sophisticated weaponry that thwarts the devilish intention and the deceitful approach to humanity (especially believers in Christ). The Word subdues all the blatant lies of the deceiver, and puts him to flight when soldiers of the Cross wage it judiciously, appropriately, or rightly in the spiritual warfare. That is one of the reasons the tempter tries all he can to distort its trustworthiness or totally annihilate it if he can. Undeniably, he cannot.

---

[134] Ibid., 89-90.

God's Word is beyond destruction for its weaponry in spiritual warfare is neither human-made nor demon-backed.

In another development, a group of scientists were humiliated and subjected to ridicule and mockery after their research and findings to number the stars proved futile and filthy in the light of the powerful and transcendent Word of God. "And He brought him forth abroad, and said, Look now toward heaven, and tell the stars, if thou be able to number them: and He said unto him, So shall thy seed be."(Gen. 15:5). Abraham (formerly Abram) had a promise of God that his offspring would be like the stars—uncountable. The following is a list of them who in their quest to number the stars became great, and deep seated liars like their father Satan (John 8:44);

> Hipparcus was a scientist who lived over 2,000 years ago. He was interested in astronomy, the study of the stars. "Now let me see, uh, 1,023, 1,024, 1,025, Yes, there are exactly 1,026 stars in the universe!" Several hundred years later in the city of Rome lived Ptolemy, who also spent much time studying the stars. He said, "There are not just 1,026 stars in the universe, I've counted them, and there are 1,056 stars!" A few years later there came along an even greater scientist named Galileo. With the help of telescope Galileo found out that there are more than 1,056 stars in the universe. In fact, the 200 inch telescope has shown that there billions of galaxies or groups of stars...There is nothing wrong with building bigger and better telescopes. They will only prove that, as God said in Jeremiah 33:22, the stars of the sky are countless.[135]

Their latest finding determines that there is no need to waste time to count them because there are billions of them—they are simply countless. If they were able to count the stars they would come out to attack God and His Word. However, God's Word is flawless and is the unique weaponry of the soldier of the Cross to wage spiritual

---

[135] Ibid., 49-51.

THE NATURE OF SPIRITUAL WARFARE

warfare against the usurper and accuser of the brethren. Denial and repudiation of the biblical truth is the burning desire of the arch enemy of God and humanity.

"In comments likely to enhance his progressive reputation, Pope Francis has written a long, open letter to Eugenio Scalfari, founder of *La Repubblica* Newspaper, stating that non-believers would be forgiven by God if they follow their consciences."[136] Is this excerpt from the Pope's open letter to Eugenio Scalfari biblically and theologically sound? No. If no, then what is the Pope telling the whole world? His theological base is in this context is misleading because no one is saved by his or her conscience. "For God so loved the world that He gave His only begotten Son, that whosoever believeth in Him should not perish, but have everlasting life" (John 3:16). Hence, Pope Francis' view on salvation is biblically and theologically heretical and repulsive.

What is the church's reaction to this misleading heresy (above)? The church is divided. What are Satan and his demonic agents' countenance to this bombshell in the church and in the world? The devil and his agents (both spiritual and human) are celebrating this excruciating attack on God and His Word. The enemy of God and His children think they have successfully waged their warfare through this false and unbiblical doctrine of salvation which distorts the biblical truth that says, "Neither is there salvation in any other: for there is none other under heaven given among men, whereby we must be saved" (Acts4:12). The power and authority of the Word of God as divine weaponry used to wage spiritual warfare, triumphs and prevails over such unfounded doctrine to give God the glory. Though some will believe Pope Francis' baseless and vague doctrine of salvation, still there are some devoted children of God (a remnant of believers in Jesus Christ) who unswervingly hold to the sound biblical doctrine of salvation through faith in Jesus Christ (John 3:36; Rom. 10:9-10; I John 5:11-12).

Dr. Murphy suggests that "while prayer is not to be seen as an additional piece of armor, it is directly connected to all Paul has

---

[136] GhanaWeb, You Don't Have to Believe in God to Go to Heaven, http://www.ghanaweb.com/GhanaHomePage/religion/artikel.php?ID=285531 (Accessed on September 12, 2013)

said from verses 10-17."[137] Prayer is indispensable for waging spiritual warfare. Prayer accentuates efficacy in waging spiritual warfare. Prayer is the wheel that moves prayer warriors and the church from victory to victory. Prayer is foundational to the development of waging victorious spiritual battle. Paul culminates his teachings on prayer by saying "Praying always with all prayer and supplication in the Spirit, and watching thereunto with all perseverance and supplication for all saints" (Eph.6:18). To emerge victorious in spiritual warfare with the hostile power and agents of Satan, the apostle Paul makes firm emphasis on the indispensible character of prayerfulness; thus Spirit-filled, faith-filled, faith-motivated, prevailing, penetrating, and persistent prayerful believers in Christ Jesus.

Further support of this concept comes from Donald Bloesch:

> Theology that is biblical and evangelical will always be nurtured by prayer. Moreover, it will give special attention to the life of prayer, since theology is inseparable from spirituality. Theology is not concerned not only with the Logos but also with the Spirit who reveals and applies the wisdom of Christ to our hearts. John Calvin refers to prayer as "the soul of faith," and indeed faith without prayer soon becomes lifeless. It is by prayer that we make contact with God. It is likewise through prayer that God communicates with us.[138]

In one of His parables concerning prayer Jesus gives a vivid and convincing illustration to this effect (Luke 18:1). Thus, Jesus Christ cautions His followers to pray without giving up or retreating because of seemingly delayed results. The Holy Spirit helps believers in Christ to travail in prayer to step into God's cause. Spirit-anointed vertical prayer equips the believer with prudence, courage, bravery, strength, insights, self control, and faith to combat the alienating

---

[137] Murphy, 412.

[138] Donald Bloesch, "Prayer," in *Evangelical Dictionary of Theology,* ed. Walter Elwell (Grand Rapids: Baker Books, 1999), 866.

hostile powers of darkness and to accelerate God's salvific plan for humanity.

Dr. George Wood says "we must exercise power in spiritual warfare with great caution, making sure that we exercise it in the right manner and against the right enemy."[139] As the enemy fights unceasingly to refuse and retard the advancement of the Kingdom, so children of the Kingdom should consciously seek to outwit him by agonizing in a ceaseless and powerful prayer life. Dr. Wood asserts "the call to prayer is a fitting end to any discussion of spiritual warfare."[140]

Neglecting or underrating Spirit-led prayer in the life of a believer is cancerous. Nothing can take the place of prayer to appropriate Christ's outstanding victory for the believer in Christ, the Church, and the Kingdom of God at large. Therefore, prayerlessness is serious negligence that exposes the believer in Christ to the fiery and deadly darts of the enemy. Prayerlessness is faithlessness. Prayerlessness diverts the attention of the believer in Christ to fight against the flesh instead of the common enemy—satanic forces. Prayerlessness initiates and culminates fierce fighting among church leaders in different local assemblies, churches, and congregations over membership. Prayer animates the dynamics and efficacy of spiritual warfare—a call for God to act in His majesty for His glory. Prayer binds believers together to wage effective warfare against the arch rival of God and the cause of His Kingdom.

Dr. James Branford has this insight to share on the poignant issue of prayer:

> One great mystery of the relationship between Christ and His church is that He involves us in His purposes. He has chosen to work through us rather than around us. This is how we understand prayer. The release of His power comes as we partner with Him, around His will, in prayer and intercession. Unfortunately, many

---

[139] George O. Wood, "The Armor of God: A Meditation on Ephesians 6:10-20," *Enrichment: Enriching and Equipping Spirit-Filled Ministers* Vol. 18, no. 3 (June 2013), 48.

[140] Ibid., 52.

spiritual leaders are more known for their external activities than their internal prayerfulness. We pray too little and work too much.[141]

Members of the kingdom of God are called to partake in His cause, "For we are his workmanship, created in Christ Jesus unto good works, which God hath before ordained that we should walk in them" (Eph. 2:10). Hence, the Spirit of God ministers to the children of God to advance the kingdom of God. Jesus affirms His active involvement in His mission with believers by giving the Great Commandment to His disciples (Matt. 28:20b). Jesus invokes His presence, power, provision, and protection through the indwelt Holy Spirit. The human flesh is inadequate to counter-confront the enemy. Prior to His ascension, Jesus reaffirmed the Father's promise concerning the coming of the Holy Spirit (Acts 1:4-8). Waging spiritual warfare with the human mind and strength without being filled, equipped, and empowered by the Holy Spirit, results in a fatal fall and defeat. There is no such doctrine that believers in Christ should sit aloof while God works around them. Church leaders tread on dangerous ground if they devote the majority of their time to only studying the Word of God and squeeze insignificant time to travail in prayer. Working with God to appropriate His cause involves ceaseless prayer—both vertically and horizontally.

I harmonize with Dr. Murphy that "prayer is too grand, too foundational, too essential, too all encompassing to be listed as just another piece of spiritual armor—despite their importance."[142] Prayer is obligatory component or ingredient in all spiritual battle against the enemy to subdue him, loose his captives, and accelerate God's passionate yearning to bring lost humanity to Himself for eternal fellowship—God's ultimate goal for humanity (Ezek. 33:3; 2 Pet. 3:9b). The essence of prayer is that it is the premise on which effective spiritual warfare and the consummation of the victory of Jesus Christ in the life of the believer in Him. Prayer is interwoven

---

[141] James T. Brantford, "Keep on Praying for All the Saints: Intercession and Spiritual Warfare," *Enrichment: Enriching, and Equipping Spirit-filled Ministers* Vol. 8, no. 3, (June 2013), 54-55.

[142] Murphy, 412.

in the whole armor of God to wage the spiritual battle against the devil with unwavering assurance of triumph.

Brantford argues that "spiritual warfare is not won through conflict resolution or strategic planning."[143] Spiritual warfare is won by the foundational activity common to every victory in the unseen realm—prayer."[144] The results of spiritual warfare determine its actual or physical manifestation. For instance, Africa is noted for its coup d'etats—usurpation of political power by the military. The main object behind the frequency of the military taking over power from elected democratic governments and subsequent overwhelming abuse of power have been discovered by Spirit-filled and prayerful church leaders in many countries of the African sub region. In some countries civil wars and ceaseless escalating ethnic conflicts jeopardize growth in social, church, and other spheres of life.

In his thesis for the Master of Arts in Military Art and Science at US Army Command and General Staff College, Lt. Col. Richard Amponsem Boateng posits that "In Africa, surrogate and civil wars, ethnic conflict and coup d'etats and territorial disputes are among the threats to peace and stability in the region."[145] Instability of government, businesses, and church life are among others that are under fierce attack and intimidation of torture and death. During such times chaos and exploitation, rapes, robbery and other nefarious social injustices occur. Some of the affected people flee for their lives into neighboring countries. Human, financial and natural resources are trampled over and affected countries become financially, professionally, and spiritually demoralized.

Despite these threats to peace and stability in Africa, Ghana has enjoyed peace and stability of government for over three decades. Why is Ghana regarded as a beacon of peace in the African sub region? The answer is the Spirit-filled, and the faith-filled prayer of the church as they come together to pray that the living God intervenes and vindicates the country from coup d'états and other

---

[143] Brantford, 54.

[144] Ibid.

[145] Richard Amponsem Boateng, "Prospects of the Economic Community of West African States Standby Force" (MAMAS, thesis, US Army Command and General Staff College, 2006), 1.

vices that disrupt the peace and harmony. "At a meeting with the leaders of Ghana Pentecostal and Charismatic Churches President Mills of Ghana reiterated that "the success of the nation was [is] not solely to human effort but through the power and help of God."[146] The demonic and deadly aroma of self-complacency, self-abasement, self-achievement, and self-sufficiency are suppressed outright with the nations well-being attributed to the sufficiency of the Almighty God.

In a similar demonic attack that suppresses and threatens peace and security of the United States of America, Al Qaeda leader Ayman al-Zawahri angrily said,

> We should bleed America economically by provoking it to continue in its massive expenditure on its security, for the weak point of America is its economy, which has already began to stagger due to military and security expenditure. Keeping America in such a state of tension and anticipation only required a few desperate attacks here and there. As we defeated it in the gang warfare in Somalia, Yemen, Iraq, and Afghanistan, so we should follow it with war…on its own land.[147]

Mapping out a military strategy with diverse and sophisticated weapons might elicit success against the terrorist plots of Al Qaeda. However, United States church leaders and their various congregations should take the initiative by coming together as a formidable squad to pray for forgiveness for the church, the executive, the judiciary, the legislature, the president, and the vice president, the people, and the land of United States for their endorsement, involvement, and promotion of sinful, abominable deeds against God (2 Chron. 7:12-16). This is spiritual warfare that calls for the mighty power of God

---

[146] Modern Ghana, http://www.modernghana.com/news/371802/1/pentecostal-and-charismatic-group-calls-on-preside.html (Accessed on October 7, 2013).

[147] Reuters, Al Qaeda Calls for Attacks Inside United States, file:///C:/Users/david/Downloads/Al%20Qaeda%20calls%20for%20attacks%20inside%20United%20States%20-%20Yahoo%20News.htm (Accessed on September 12, 2013).

through His Church to counter-attack satanic forces that are backing and pushing this act of inhuman and insolence to God erroneously asumed by Islam as holy war *jihad*. "Except the LORD keeps the city, the watchmen waketh but in vain" (Ps. 127:1b).

Reliance on self expertise and blatant disregard for the self existence, prominence, providence, and protection of the One True God (the Creator of the heaven and the earth) propels the United States and all its allies into perpetual mockery and fragility in the eyes of devilish forces through terrorism and other future inhuman operations. Though the Al Qaeda leader Ayman al- Zawahri has laid threats of destroying United States if the people the United States will indisputable recognition the existence and sovereignty of God, accept the Christian Holy Bible as the infallible and authoritative Word of God, confess their blatant disobedience to God, and allow God and His Word to be the center of life beginning from individuals, marriages, families, various levels of educational institutions, state governments, to the White House. Triumph awaits United States If the people of United States will confess their inadequacies to suppress the arch enemy, expose his wicked intentions and their minds and hearts, voluntarily and vehemently reject and renounce his rebellious and abominable deeds like gay marriage and lesbianism, and cleave to God's moral standards. Triumph awaits United States if the remnant of the Kingdom of God in the nation will travail in prayer. I am not talking about recitation of prayer *status quo*, non-biblical based prayer, faithless prayer, and irreverence to God prayer. I mean agonized faith-filled, faith-persevered prayer (James 5:16) with hearts full of remorse and penitence, and absolute recognition and acceptance of the exclusive lordship of JESUS CHRIST as the Son of God (John 14:12-14).

"Prayer is the key to effective warfare with high-level, cosmic powers of evil."[148] Prayer is dependence of the finite human being on the infinite Being. Prayer is not about merely reciting words, but being led by the Spirit of God to express emptiness and insufficiency of self, and needfulness of God's mercy, forgiveness, healing, restoration of spiritual fervor, cleaving to biblical and theological

---

[148] Murphy, 412.

definition and practices of the sacred institution of marriage and family ties. Prayer is a mark of humility and obedience to God and His Word. Prayer demonstrates communion and alignment with the infinite God to fulfill His plan. Prayer diverts attention from challenges or problems at stake and rather focuses on the magnificence and awesomeness of God.

> In her profound contribution in *Enrichment,* Dr. Elizabeth Grant advocates that; The success of the kingdom of darkness in our cities, nation, and the world is inevitable—If God's people avoid, shirk, ignore or timidly refuse to engage in spiritual battle against Satan's systemic schemes. But victory for the kingdom of God in our cities is divinely ordained if God's people discern His strategic purposes, intercede against systems of injustice, and boldly proclaim Christ's victory over evil.[149]

The Christian Holy Bible explicitly talks about the triumph of Jesus Christ at Calvary over all evil systems and structures with the arch enemy who invented and initiated its action (Matt. 28:18; Acts 2:22-24, 36; Col. 2:15; I John 3:8). Though Jesus won the war against Satanic forces on behalf of humanity it is appropriated by exclusively accepting Jesus Christ as the Son of the living God— born again in Christ (John 3: 3-5). No weapon is adequate to triumph in spiritual warfare than the one approved of God. Neither is there any human strategy, theory or philosophy that is adequate enough to suppress Satanic forces (2 Cor. 10:3-5).

If the community of faith in Christ Jesus therefore spearheads the warfare with humble obedience, heart-felt, persistence, and Spirit-led prayer in the name of Jesus Christ (John 14:12-14)—not in the name of Mary, Allah, Mohamed, Buddha, Confucius, nation, president, billionaire, a particular church, or any other name—then the victory of Christ Jesus is assured in personal life, family life,

---

[149] Elizabeth Grant, "Proclaiming Christ's Victory Over Unjust Social Structures and Practices," *Enrichment: Enriching and Equipping Spirit-filled Ministers* Vol. 8, no. 3, (June 2013), 65.

the church, the community, nations, and the world at large. By waging the warfare with humble obedience, reverence, and recognition to God and His statutes then, satanic strongholds and powers behind terrorism would be subdued under the Name above all names, Jesus Christ.

CHAPTER 4

OLD TESTAMENT ANTECEDENT OF "THE KINGDOM OF GOD"

"Though the term "the Kingdom of God" is not expressed in the Old Testament canonical books the idea is present throughout the Old Testament."[150] The kingship of God transcends time and space likewise His Kingdom (the Kingdom of God). *"For God is the King of all the earth"* (Ps. 47:7). Caragounis further elaborates:

> In a number of instances Yahweh is presented as king (Deut 9:26 [LXX]; I Sam12:12; Ps 24:10 [LXX 23:10]; 29:10 [LXX 28:10]; Is 6:5; 33:22; Zeph 3:15; Zech14:16, 17). At other places he is ascribed as a royal throne (Ps 9:4 [LXX 9:5]; 45:6 [LXX 44:7]; 47:8 [LXX 46:9]; Is 6:1; 66:1; Ezek 1:26; Sir 1:8) while occasionally his continuous or future reign is affirmed (Ps 10:16 [LXX 9:37]; 146:10 LXX 145:10]; Is 24:23; Wis 3:8). In fact Psalm 22:28 (MT 22:29; LXX 21:29) says "the kingdom" (hamm'luka; LXX basileia) belongs to the Lord.[151]

---

[150] Caragounis, "Kingdom of God/Kingdom of Heaven," 417.
[151] Ibid.

There is no king like Yahweh, and there is no king besides Him. As Creator (Heb.1:10), His reign has no beginning and end. The Kingdom of God dominates all temporary kingdoms. His creative ability and capability attest to His kingship for whatever exists— human beings, spirits, powers, dominions, and thrones are subject to Him for no one competes with Him, His acts, His attributes and His kingship.

From Creation to the Tower of Babel

The King of the Kingdom is also the Creator of the universe. The biblical truth of God as Creator of the universe thwarts "the so-called evolutionary philosophies...that have no logical derivation from views of how God chose to create his world – let alone of why he did so."[152] The Psalmist also says, "The earth is the LORD'S, and the fullness thereof; the world, and they that dwell therein, For he hath founded it upon the seas, and established it upon the waters" (Ps. 24:1-2). Charles Darwin's theory of evolution[153] and others that try to distort the biblical truth and theological truth of creation are part of the devil's agents to deny the undeniable truth of creation.

With this foundational truth established about the doctrine of creation, then the question arises, Who is the author of spiritual warfare?

Twelftree shares more on Satan;

> Origen equated Lucifer (Is. 14:12-15) with Satan, who with the powers revolted and fell from heaven because of pride. Augustine followed Origen, but not in thinking that the devil could be reconciled to God. Over against Anslem, Abelard believed that the atonement had nothing to do with the devil. Thomas Aquinas who held that the devil, who is the cause of all sin, was once probably the very highest angel who, through pride, fell immediately after creation,

---

[152] Caragounis, "Kingdom of God/Kingdom of Heaven," 178.
[153] Ibid.

seducing those who followed him to become his subjects.[154]

Thus, the devil is the author of spiritual warfare. He rebelled and battled alongside his allies against God and His cause. After his insolent revolt against his Creator, he was deposed from his place of prestige that was given to him by the same God against whom he battled. This first revolt of the devil took place before the fall of Adam and Eve—"How art thou fallen from heaven, O Lucifer, son of the morning!" (Is. 14:12a) The passage from the prophet Isaiah conveys the theological idea that Lucifer lost his place because of his own initiated battle in the heavens. I vouch that Satan, and not God, is the initiator and inventor of war. The devil is a usurper who wanted to dominate God and his kingdom. However, the sovereign God demonstrated His omnipotence over the rebellious creature (Lucifer) by casting him from heaven. This event marks the beginning of spiritual warfare. Lucifer's rebellion against the Kingdom of God gave birth to his fall. Lucifer exerts his bitterness upon humanity after his fall.

Robert Sims puts it this way:

> Since the fall of Lucifer, that angel of light and the son of the morning, there has been no respite in the bitter Battle of the Ages. Night and day Lucifer, the master craftsman of the devices of darkness, labors to thwart God's plan of the ages. We can find inscribed on every page of human history the consequences of the evil brought to fruition by the powers of darkness with the devil in charge.[155]

---

[154] G. H Twelftree, "Devil and Demons," in *New Dictionary of Theology*, ed. Sinclair Ferguson (Downers Grove: InterVarsity Press, 1988), 197.

[155] What is Spiritual Warfare, "A Definition of Spiritual Warfare," http://www.battlefocused.org/articles/what-is-spiritualwarfare/#.U (Accessed of August 17, 2013).

OLD TESTAMENT ANTECEDENT OF "THE KINGDOM OF GOD"

John the revelator says "...And the great dragon was cast out, that old serpent called the Devil, and Satan...Woe to the inhabitants of the earth and of the sea! For the devil is come down unto you, having great wrath, because he knoweth that he hath but a short time" (Rev. 12:7-12). In his insightful book, *The Handbook of Spiritual Warfare,* Dr. Ed

Murphy asserts "Satan's tactics and his strategy have not changed since the Garden of Eden."[156]

"The major focus of spiritual warfare as experienced by humanity, begins with Genesis chapter three, where the talking and seducing serpent enters to shatter the hope of Adam and Eve." [157] The devil capitalized on the innocence and fragility of Eve and Adam by launching spiritual warfare against God and His cause. The deceitful move of the serpent subjected Adam and Eve's expulsion from the Garden of Eden. "The Garden of Eden, means "to enrich, make abundant" or "garden of abundance."[158] Thus, Adam and Eve fell from a place of perfection, enrichment, and abundance. The devil's plan to attack "the Kingdom of God" through Adam and Eve was very successful. He changed their place of abode, and he changed their designation from obedient servants of God to rebellious, disobedient, and doomed human beings.

The deceiver also caused Adam to accuse God, thus, "the woman whom thou gavest to be with me, she gave me of the tree, and I did eat" (Gen. 3:12). It seems Adam was telling God that "when I was here alone, nothing wrong happened to me, but after you gave me "the bone of my bone, and the flesh of my flesh" (Gen. 2:23), she lured me to disobey your word that says "But the tree of the knowledge of good and evil, "thou shalt not eat of it; for the in the day that thou eatest thereof thou shalt surely die" (Gen. 2:17). I perceive that Adam and Eve had an escalating conflict and misunderstanding that still creeps in to marital life with broken homes, unfaithfulness, rudeness, jealousy, friction, dissatisfaction, apathy, rampant divorce, adultery,

---

[156] Murphy, 33.

[157] Ibid., 34.

[158] John H. Walton, "Eden, Garden of," in *Dictionary of Old Testament Pentateuch,* ed. T. Desmond Alexander (Downers Grove: InterVarsity Press, 2003), 202.

homosexuality, and other immoral practices that persistently seek to redefine and pervert the sacred institution of marriage.

"Becoming aware of what he did to our first parents, and how he did it, will serve to forewarn and arm us for the spiritual battle we all face here and now."[159] Ascertaining the biblical and theological truth that the whole human race comes through Adam and Eve, then it is equally significant to admit that human beings (irrespective of color, language, stature, ethnicity, nationality, gender, and societal status) never evolve from any species of animals. The human race keeps multiplying through the first parents (Adam and Eve). Extremely furious, crafty, and evil-consumed Satan cunningly confronted the first parents, deceitfully disengaged them from biblical truth, wantonly devastated their relationship with one another, and finally disconnected them outright from enjoying the blessedness of Creator God.

Dr. Murphy summarizes the consequences of the fatal fall of humanity as follows:

> The first was subjective: The Fall altered man's dispositional complex and changed his attitude toward God (Gen. 3:7-16). Man once found his supreme delight in the presence of God: now he flees from God's face. The second was objective: The call changed God's relationship to man. The wrathful aspect of God's nature hinted at in Genesis 2:17 was revealed after Genesis 3:9). The third was cosmic: All creation was "injured." The ground was cursed because of the Fall (Gen. 3:17-19). The fourth result was racial: Adam and Eve's fall affected the whole human race. The fifth was death.[160]

The spiritual battle in the Garden of Eden between the serpent and Adam and Eve affected the totality of humanity and creation culminated with spiritual death and physical death. Satan's fierce

---

[159] Murphy, 33.
[160] Ibid., 46.

battle with the human race continues until God completes "the new heaven and the new Earth" (Rev. 21:1). The devil dominated the first offspring (Cain) of the first parents (Adam and Eve), and profusely stirred God's anger: "... when they were in the field, that Cain rose up against Abel his brother, and slew him" (Gen. 4:8b). The spiritual battle against God and His kingdom is ongoing, and the devil who initiated this battle fights unceasingly against humanity, especially believers in Jesus Christ.

"The earth also was corrupt before God, and the earth was filled with violence" (Gen. 6:11); therefore God purposed to cause a flood to destroy the whole earth and everything in it, with the exception of Noah, his family, and two of "every living thing of all flesh" (Gen. 6:13-21). "Thus, did Noah, according to all that God commanded him, so did he" (Gen. 6:22). Favored Noah took God at his word, conveying the biblical and theological truth and expectation that children of the kingdom of God are people of faith and are obedient to God and His word. "The righteous and holy God does not compromise sin because "sin sets up a diabolic circle around the soul"[161] and warrants its death. Sin is primarily disobedience to God and His word, but those who strive to live lives of obedience and surrender to God enjoy the blessedness of God. "In Genesis the survivors were Noah and his family accompanied by animals by twos (unclean) and sevens (clean)."[162] As a reward of his persistent striving to please God, Noah and his family were shielded and protected from the historic judgment of flood which covered the surface of the whole earth (Gen. 8:1).

Atheists and skeptics might doubt the truthfulness of the historic flood in the days of Noah. However, besides biblical and theological proofs, Dr. Walton provides three additional Ancient Near Eastern sources of proof under the title *Flood:*

> There are three major documents from Mesopotamia that offer an account of the Flood. The earliest, a Sumerian fragment of about seventy lines was found

---

[161] Walter Hollenweger, *The Pentecostals* (Peabody: Hendrickson Publishers, 1988), 379.

[162] John H. Walton, "Flood," in *Dictionary of the Old Testament Pentateuch,* ed. T. Desmond Alexander (Downer's Grove: InterVarsity Press, 2003), 317.

at Nippur and is generally dated to seventeenth century B.C. (published by M. Civil in Lambert and Millard). It was combined by Jacobsen with two other fragments into a hypothetical composition he entitled "The Eridu Genesis" (Hess and Tsumura, 129-42; COS 1.158.513-15). A roughly contemporary account in Akkadian, the Atrahasis Epic, contains and account of the creation of humankind as well as the flood (COS 1.130.450-52; Lambert and Millard). The third account of the flood is found in tablet 11 of the Gilgamesh Epic. The initial discovery of this epic was in the Ashurbanipal's library at Nineveh. This copy dates to the seventh century B.C. Subsequent discoveries and analyses have allowed the origins of the Gilgamesh Epic to be traced through the various sources from which it was compiled.[163]

The enemy's aggressive dominance over the descendants of Noah grew worse in their defiance of God's word. This time the enemy worked through the descendants of Ham, Shem, and Japheth. Prior to their act of disobedience to God's word, God spoke to Noah and his sons saying, "Be fruitful and multiply, and replenish the earth" (Gen. 9:1). Like Eve who defied God and chose to obey the serpent in the Garden of Eden, the descendants of Shem, Ham, and Japheth disobeyed God's instruction to them (Gen. 11:1-4). The deceiver succeeded in trapping the families of the sons of Noah to act contrary to the command of God (Gen. 9:1). In their counter estimation, they wanted to build a tall tower that reached up to heaven, confine themselves in the tower by not scattering contrary to God's word, and more outrageously to abase themselves—thus, to build a kingdom for themselves as opposed to the eternal kingdom of God. Puffed up with satanic thoughts and dreams, their futile imagination and arrogant intentions propelled them to become allies of Lucifer, and enemies of God (James 4:4). The enemy of humanity is here in the spiritual hiding behind the scene to carry out his deadly

---

[163] Ibid,. 315.

heart's desire, to deprive humanity of aligning themselves with the Creator God who yearns always to have harmonious communion with humanity (created in His own image).

This move of the children of men in Genesis chapter 11 brought the name "the Tower of Babel." Osborne says, "Babel is the name given to the city that, according to the story in Genesis 11:1-9, was constructed in the plain of the land of Shinar and whose construction led God to confuse the builders' language and to scatter them."[164] Their dreams were shattered, in the futility of their thinking they were halted, they were confused, and there was unexpected dissemination of their language and speech (Gen. 11:5-9).

"The Tower of Babel, indeed Babylon itself, takes us right into the arena of terrible spiritual warfare."[165] Infringement on God and His Kingdom is warfare backed by Lucifer. The building of the Tower of Babel is no exception. "Both the Tower and the city are symbols of religious humanism, idolatry, polytheism, and defiance of God."[166] The enemy knows that God is holy and righteous; He frowns at detestable acts of humanity, and He does not condone sin. There is no doubt that the deceiver was the spirit behind building the Tower of Babel.

"While Satan's tactics might change, his goal is always the same—to lead humanity to rebel against the lordship of God and to serve Satan, who sees himself as his own god, or by serving false gods."[167] The sin of Babel is a symbol that connotes the idea of creating god structures and systems inclined to satisfy the demonic lust of pride and self abasement. Eve wanted to be like God (Gen. 3:5); and the children of Shem, Ham, and Japheth wanted to build a kingdom like God and make a name for themselves (Gen.11:4). Human beings are always influenced by the devil to indulge in acts of vain glory and arrogance and suffer the consequences of their disobedience to God.

---

[164] William Osborne, "Babel," in *Dictionary of Old Testament Pentateuch*, ed. T. Desmond Alexander (Downers Grove: InterVarsity Press, 2003), 73.

[165] Murphy, 230.

[166] Ibid.

[167] Ibid.

The Patriarchs

According to Webster, a patriarch is one of the scriptural fathers of the human race or of the Hebrew people."[168] Dr. Liefeld says "the term, recalling the Old Testament patriarchs were heads of their families or of tribes, is an ecclesiastical title used in both Roman Catholic and Eastern Orthodox churches."[169]

Abram who was later called Abraham and his wife Sarai later named Sarah by God were the first and original parents from whom God built the Hebrew race—a people in whom God would fulfill His promise to bless all nations. As Abraham is regarded as the progenitor of the Israelite nation,[170] so Sarai or Sarah was the matriarch of the Israelite nation. According to Merriam-Webster, the word matriarch means a mother who is head and ruler of her family and descendants.[171] Dr. Branch says, Abraham was the first patriarch and she [Sarah] the first matriarch in the biblical text.[172] The patriarch (Abraham) and the matriarch (Sarah) are the couple God approved to raise a new generation of people in the cause of building His Kingdom.

"The enormity of what happened at Babel in Gen 11, leads God to initiate a new strategy in dealing with the human race: the choice of Abraham and God's promise to him."[173] After confounding the languages and speeches of those who wanted to build the tower of Babel and subsequently scattering them throughout the surface of the earth (Gen. 11:1-9), God called Abram from Ur in the land of the Chaldeans (Gen. 11:28) to continue building His everlasting Kingdom of God (Gen. 12:1-2).

---

[168] Merriam-Webster, *Merriam-Webster's Collegiate Dictionary*, (Springfield: Merriam-Webster Incorporated, 2005), 908.

[169] Walter Liefeld, "Patriarch," in *Evangelical Dictionary of Theology*, ed. Walter A. Elwell (Grand Rapids: Baker Books, 1999), 829.

[170] Ibid.

[171] Merriam-Webster, *Merriam-Webster*, 766.

[172] Robin Branch, "Sarah," in *Dictionary of Old Testament Pentateuch*, ed. T. Desmond Alexander (Downers Grove: InterVarsity, 2003), 733.

[173] William Osborne, "Babel" In *Dictionary of Old Testament Pentateuch*, ed. T. Desmond Alexander (Downers Grove: InterVarsity Press, 2003), 73.

God commanded Abraham leave his comfort zone and sojourn to an unknown place. Though God promised an enormous package of blessings for Abram, the command to move from the known to the unknown is not easy for a human being to understand and proceed wholeheartedly. Satan attempts to hinder people from obeying God's voice in similar issue. Missionaries and other servants of Christ Jesus who obey God's voice and leave their comfort zones to uncomfortable zones for the sake of Christ and the Gospel are bountifully rewarded for their selfless intuition and genuine devotion to fulfill their respective calling to advance God's heartbeat—the mission of God, *missio Dei*.

Though Sarai was barren (Gen. 11:30) God promised to bless Abram. Abram and Sarai probably contemplated on their impotence with regard to their ages and childbearing in contrast to the pronounced blessing. In their contemplation, the enemy also inflicted them with doubt and confusion with the aim to accuse God of a falsehood—as he normally does to captivate the whims and caprice of humanity. Abram and Sarai went to Egypt because of a severe famine (Gen. 12:10). The enemy capitalized on Abram's insecurity and the spiritual battle ensued (Gen. 12:11-15).

"This episode in the patriarch's career is a rather unfortunate one: Abraham places both himself and his family in grave peril."[174] The liar succeeded in injecting the spirit of fear and doubt into the life of Abram and his wife Sarai. The same devil put lust in the eyes and hearts of Pharaoh and his servants, causing Sarai to be taken to the house of the Egyptian leader (pharaoh). The spiritual war intensified to the extent that God had to intervene to prove Satan wrong in his intentions and defeated in his (Satan) warfare against God's newfound friend Abram and his wife Sarai.

God's intervention held back the tempest of immorality and adultery that arose in the heart and mind of Pharaoh through the cunning strategy of the devil. Pharaoh seemingly had Satan–sugar-coated pill to swallow to remedy his dubious lust. Only divine intervention averts disaster and keeps the promise of descendants

---

[174] Peter R. Williamson, "Abraham," in *Dictionary of Old Testament Pentateuch*, ed. T. Desmond Alexander (Downers Grove, InterVarsity Press, 2003), 9.

alive. [175] Abram's lie coupled with Pharaoh's escalated sexual lust was counter-attacked by God's sovereign power and His faithfulness to His promise to bless all nations through the seed of Abram, not Pharaoh (Gen. 12:18-13:1).

Though the Bible does not say what actually happened to Pharaoh to motivate him to anxiously question and make such strong statements and commands of Abram. Pharaoh could not refuse God's command or paralyze God's plan to bless the whole world through the seed of Abram. The Covenant-keeping God always fulfills His promises. Though Abram and Sarai were advanced in years, the Creator of humanity promised to work through human incapability and inability to prove to the whole creation that indeed His sovereignty transcends all natural, spiritual, physical, and other dimensions to fulfill His salvific plan for humanity. Abram left Egypt with all he had. God rescued fear-dominated Abram from the shackles of shame, sleeplessness, and faithlessness.

Murphy says that "during their lifetime, the great patriarchs Abraham and Isaac and their families lived in the midst of the polytheism and idolatry of Canaan but remained true to God."[176] Yes, Canaan was polluted with diverse immoral practices including polytheism and idolatry but that is where God wanted His servant Abram and his descendants to live and possess as inheritance to attest to His faithful promise in building His eternal Kingdom amidst persistent spiritual warfare waged by the arch enemy Satan.

"Genesis 16 relates how Abraham himself complicates matters when, at his wife's bidding he obtains (at the age of eighty-six, Gen 16:16) a surrogate heir through Hagar, Sarah's Egyptian slave girl."[177] Satan's wicked initiative and dubious influence was very vivid in this unfortunate act of Sarai and her husband Abram (Gen. 16:1-12). This is the second time in the history of humanity that a husband followed a weak and naïve suggestion and brought a severe snare and lifetime punishment upon the human race. The first

---

[175] Ibid.

[176] Murphy, 233.

[177] Ibid.

occurred in the Garden of Eden (Gen. 3) and the second in the land of Canaan (Gen. 16).

Are wives a snare to husbands? No. In God's divine power and incomparable wisdom He made a woman from the rib of man and gave her to man as "a help meet for him" (Gen. 2;18). Do not men also have a will to object to their wives' Satan-led decisions? They have, but James gives an antidote to avert such hasty inclination that leads to disaster, depravity, and destruction of both vertical and horizontal relationships: "Wherefore, my beloved brethren, let everyman be swift to hear, slow to speak, slow to wrath" (James 1:19). Abram's hasty affirmation of Sarai adds more injury to the chronic wound caused by Adam's similar swift inclination to Eve's treacherous enticement suggested and motivated by the serpent—a rebellious and indelible mark in the life of humanity through all generations.

The result of the faithless proposal made by Sarai and welcomed by Abram, was the birth of Ishmael by Hagar—"a wild man" (Gen. 16:12). "And Hagar bore Abram a son: and Abram called his son's name, which Hagar bare, Ishmael (Gen. 16:15). "The birth of Ishmael leaves open the possibility that the programmatic agenda of Gen. 12: 1-3 will be realized through Abraham and Hagar's son."[178] The deceiver celebrated his wicked scheme to impede the plan and promise of God for and through Abram as God builds the everlasting Kingdom. The enemy thought Ishmael was the original seed God promised Abram. Rather, Ishmael was a counterfeit of the original seed of Abram; a violent controversialist the devil used to advance his treacherous and temporal kingdom of deception, darkness, and death he (Satan) and his allies war against the Kingdom of God through aggressive and unceasing assault. Ishmael was a violent vessel to perpetuate the spiritual warfare waged by the arch enemy against God and humanity.

The LORD appeared to Abram and cautioned him to wholeheartedly obey His word and be justified. God covenanted with Abram, changed his name from Abram to Abraham (a father of many nations), and promised Abraham bountiful blessings that

---

[178] Williamson, "Abraham," 10.

extend to his offspring from generation to generation. Though God mentioned the gift of the land of Canaan to the offspring of Abraham He reassigned it to the seed of Abraham as part of His promise. God promised Abraham that He would be the God of his descendants—theocratic rule (Gen. 17:1-8).

Concerning the covenant God told Abraham, "This is my covenant, which ye shall keep, between me and you and thy seed after thee; Every man child among you shall be circumcised" (Gen. 17:10). As a token of the covenant between God and Abraham the latter was commanded to circumcise all children (male) born in his house on the eighth day from generation to generation, and all males bought with money in his household as an everlasting covenant (Gen. 17: 11-13).

"Sarah indeed conceived and bore a child at approximately age ninety; her husband was approximately one hundred."[179] "it is through the lawful wife that God's promise of progeny, land, greatness, and blessings comes."[180] God fulfilled His promise of the birth of Isaac through Sarah and Abraham (Gen. 21:1-5) in the midst of escalating spiritual warfare waged by the devil.

God gives faith as a unique gift to subjects of the Kingdom to unwittingly and actively walk with Him in advancing His cause. "The greatest test of Abraham's faith came when God instructed him to sacrifice Isaac on Mt. Moriah."[181] In the course of time, God told Abraham, "Take now thy son, thine only son Isaac, whom thou lovest, and get thee into the land of Moriah; and offer him there for a burnt offering upon one of the mountains of which I will tell thee of" (Gen. 22: 2). Abraham took God at His word and went with Isaac and one of his (Abraham) servants to Moriah—a demonstration of a poignant and penetrating faith in God and His word.

"This experience of nearly sacrificing his only son, placed Abraham in the position of God the Father, who sent his one and only Son to Mt. Calvary, not far from Mt. Moriah (II Chr. 3:1)."[182]

---

[179] Branch, "Sarah," 734.

[180] Ibid.

[181] Marten Woudstra, "Abraham," in *Evangelical Dictionary of Theology,* ed. Walter Elwell (Grand Rapids: Baker Books, 1999), 7.

[182] Woudstra, "Abraham," 7.

God the Father gave His only Son Jesus Christ to the world (John 3:16), as a sin offering (2Cor. 5:21). There is similarity in these two sacrifices, though the sacrifice of Isaac does not take away the sin of the world he was Abraham's only son like Jesus Christ being was the only son of the Father in Heaven. Further dissimilarity in these two events is that Jesus Christ was crucified for the sins of humanity, and on the third day God resurrected Him (I Cor. 15:3-4) to justify all sinners who confess Him as Lord and Savior (Rom. 10:9-10).

Another dissimilarity is that God miraculously provided a ram as a substitute to Isaac, but in the case of Jesus Christ He gave Himself a ransom (I Tim. 2:5)—a substitute for wayward humanity. God's approval always requires humble obedience—the epitome of reverence and radical faith in Him. Abraham proved his genuine and thorough obedience to God and His word, which unwittingly moved God to supernaturally provide for Abraham.

From here, the event of God building His Kingdom is focused on Isaac, divine heir of Abraham (his father). "The search for a wife for Isaac (Gen. 24) is the longest narrative in the entire book (i.e., 67 verses)."[183] A few of them will be discussed briefly in the following paragraph. The death of Sarah and Abraham (the parents of Isaac) was not the end of the God's gracious dealing with Abraham and his seed through whom all nations and peoples are blessed. The covenant-keeping God continued to build His eternal Kingdom through Isaac. It would be recalled that "…Isaac was forty years when he took Rebekah to wife, the daughter of Bethuel the Syrian of Padanaram, the sister to Laban the Syrian" (Gen. 25:20). Isaac interceded on behalf of his wife Rebekah, because she was barren (Gen. 25:21a).

"After a twenty year wait for children, Isaac's prayer is answered in the birth of twin sons to his beloved wife, Rebekah (Gen. 25:27-34)."[184] "Prenatally they struggled within Rebekah, a harbinger of their struggle throughout their lives and the future history of their respective progenies."[185] Rebekah inquired of the Lord about what

---

[183] A. Luter and Sheri Klouda, "Isaac," in *Dictionary of Old Testament Pentateuch*, ed. T. Desmond Alexander (Downers Grove: InterVarsity Press, 2003), 448.

[184] Ibid., 448.

[185] Richard Rigsby "Jacob," in *Dictionary of Old Testament Pentateuch*, ed. T. Desmond Alexander (Downers Grove: InterVarsity Press, 2003), 462.

was the outcome of the unusual struggle in her womb. And the Lord said, "Two nations are in thy womb, and two manner of people shall be separated from the bowels; and one people shall be stronger than the other people; and the elder shall serve the younger" (Gen. 25:23)." "In God's appointed time, Rebekah, the wife of Isaac gave birth to twin brothers (Gen. 25: 24) probably at Beer-lahai-roi at about 2006 BC."[186]

The battle begun in the womb of Rebekah, and the picture is vivid even at their (Esau and Jacob) birth with Jacob holding the heel of his senior twin brother (Gen. 25:25-26). The enemy capitalized on the weaknesses of Isaac and Rebekah to have extraordinary love for Esau and Jacob respectively. The spiritual warfare was intensified as Satan aggressively sought to nourish the biases of Isaac and Jacob (Gen. 25:27-28). Obviously Esau and Jacob were not ignorant about their parents' preferential treatments of them. "As they grew, their differences became manifest."[187] Thus, the dividing wall between these twins (two nations) grew stronger, thicker, and taller. The arch enemy of humanity especially people called and chosen by God to play a significant role in building the kingdom of God intensely nourished their self ego to excel his wicked agenda of havoc, hatred, humiliation, and hindrance to the cause of God.

When Isaac knew that his time to die was approaching, he called Esau his senior son and appealed to him to prepare a nice dish for him to eat so he (Isaac) could bless him before his death (Gen. 27:1-4). "Under normal circumstances, the firstborn son received certain inherited rights, including a double portion of the material inheritance, family headship with special emphasis on spiritual leadership and the father's "deathbed" blessing."[188] Rebekah overheard Isaac's advice to Esau, conveyed the message to Jacob (the one she loved more), and devised a cunning strategy to rob Esau of his blessing from his father Isaac (Gen. 27: 5-12). Satan, the deceiver, was the initiator and craftsman who dominated and deceived Rebekah to

---

[186] Ibid.,

[187] Ibid.,

[188] Ibid.

persuade Jacob in the wicked scheme to usurp Esau's presupposed blessing and inheritance (Gen. 27:9-17).

The spiritual battle was nearing its fulfillment—Rebekah's heart's desire was to divert her son Esau's blessing to her son Jacob. Rebekah and Jacob "deliberately deceived Isaac by Jacob's impersonation of his brother, by direct falsehood and by subterfuge."[189] Rebekah assisted her son Isaac to wear Esau's "field-smelling" clothes, put hairy goat's skin around Jacob's hand and necks, and subtly "pushed" him (Jacob) to climax that outrageous and godless deal (Gen. 27:9-17). Hence, Isaac was deceived to pronounce blessings upon Jacob the usurper (Gen. 27:26-29).

"The blessing included promises of fertility of the earth, supremacy over other nations, mastery over Esau and his progeny and a special promise that those who blessed Jacob will be blessed, and those who cursed Jacob will be cursed."[190] Rebekah and her son Jacob accomplished their burning desire; they sabotaged shortsighted Isaac with a false presentation, and finally stripped naïve and presumptuous Esau of his birthright. Esau had previously sworn an oath and sold his birthright to Jacob for food (Gen. 25:29-34).

Esau who did not know what his own mother Rebekah and his junior twin brother Jacob had conspired to strip him of his blessing by deceiving his father Isaac also presented his savory meal to his father Isaac. "And Isaac his father said unto him, Who art thou? And he said, I am thy son, thy firstborn, Esau" (Gen. 27:32). The devil (chief antagonist) knocked the heads of Isaac, Rebekah, Esau, and Jacob together. The spiritual battle reached an alarming stage that creeps through from generation to generation. Chaos and commotion, rage and revenge, and hostility and havoc, depression and disposition loomed in the four corners of Isaac's family. What lay ahead for them and their descendants?

"Esau resolved to kill Jacob at the earliest possible opportunity, but he determined to postpone the murder until after the demise of their father."[191] Rebekah was very alarmed when she heard this

---

[189] Ibid., 462-463.

[190] Ibid., 463.

[191] Ibid.,

fierce pronouncement by Esau against her beloved Jacob. Rebekah "advised Jacob to flee to Haran in Paddan-aram to take refuge with her brother Laban, justifying her counsel by urging Jacob not to marry one of the local Canaanite women, as Esau had done, but to seek a wife among his own people."[192] As an accomplice of Jacob in his supplanting venture, Rebekah did what she could do to relocate Jacob from the vicinity of Esau.

Rebekah knew that Esau would take the life of her dear son Jacob so she summoned him and said, "Now therefore, my son, obey my voice; and arise, flee thou to Laban my brother in Haran (Gen. 27:43). Jacob's impromptu exit to Laban was the best choice for Rebekah. Moreover, endogamy (marrying within a select group) seems to have been the recommended procedure during patriarchal times."[193] Marrying a woman among the Canaanites as Esau did was not the best plan for Jacob, so Rebekah warned her beloved not to make that mistake. "Jacob's flight occurred when he was about seventy-seven years old."[194] Before Jacob set out to Laban his father Isaac also called him, "and blessed him (Gen. 28:1). Jacob took the advice of his parents and proceeded to Laban at Padan-aram (Gen. 28:7).

"Jacob would have travelled over the central ridge route from Beer-she-ba through Hebron, through Bethlehem, past Jerusalem, and on through Gibeah, Mizpah and Bethel (also called Luz), where he had a dream of a ladder –more likely a staircase—reaching to heaven with angels ascending and descending (Gen. 28:10-22)."[195] The schemer is seen here paving his way through to find shelter, refuge, and greener pastures as reward for his dubious act to Esau. The covenant-keeping God revealed Himself in a dream to Jacob on his way to Laban (Gen. 28:18-22).

As a heir of the promise of God through Abraham and Isaac Jacob renamed the town of Luz, calling it Bethel ("House of God").[196]

---

[192] Ibid.,

[193] Ibid.,

[194] Ibid.

[195] Ibid.

[196] Ibid.,

Fear-consumed Jacob advocated for the sovereign providence and protection of the God of his fathers. Jacob anticipated the peace of God to suppress and dominate his restlessness as a result of his despicable act to his twin brother Esau. Run-away Jacob promised to fulfill his obligation as a believer in the God of Abraham and Isaac by giving God a tenth of whatever God would provide for his upkeep.

Laban welcomed Jacob into his home and said, "Surely thou art my bone and my flesh" (Gen. 29:14). "After Jacob spent a month in Laban's house, his uncle inquired what wages Jacob needed to be paid."[197] In place of wages Jacob requested to serve his uncle Laban for seven years for Rachel the younger daughter (Gen. 29:18). After completing the seven year contract in exchange for Rachel, the enemy waged war again with one of his tricks—deception. "During the wedding ceremony at the close of that period, Laban surreptitiously substituted Leah for Rachael, excusing his behavior on the basis of the custom of the country."[198] What was the reaction of Jacob? "What is it that you have done unto me? Did not I serve with thee for Rachel? Wherefore thou hast beguiled me? (Gen. 28:25b). Did he remember his deceit against Esau? Jacob the supplanter might remember his historic case initiated by his mother Rebekah that crushed the blessing of Esau and ignited in him bitterness, rage, murderous threats, and resentment against Jacob.

"In light of Jacob's deceit of his father and brother, it is particularly ironic that his father-in-law cheated him, not just once, but consistently during the twenty years they lived together."[199] Though Jacob served his uncle Laban twenty years (fourteen years for thy Leah and Rachel and six years for cattle [Gen. 31:41]), the returns or turnout was enormous, but still the emotional torture and of fear of Esau was vivid and always fresh in the eyes, mind, and heart of "fugitive" Jacob who prepared to go back to Canaan.

"And Jacob went on his way, and the angels of God met him" (Gen. 32:1). "Just as the first of these angelic experiences had led

---

[197] Ibid.,

[198] Ibid.,.

[199] Ibid.

Jacob to name the place Bethel, so this second angelic manifestation led him to name the place Mahanaim ("Two Camps").[200] In another development Jacob "wrestled a man with him until the breaking of the day." (Gen. 32:24). Jacob's persistent zeal for God's blessing was commended. "And he said, Thy name shall be called no more Jacob, but Israel: for as a prince hast thou power with God and men, and hast prevailed" (Gen. 32:28). Thus, the angel of God changed Jacob's name to "Israel ("Striver with God" or, less likely, Prince of God")."[201]

"Following this remarkable encounter, Jacob, named the place, near the fords of the Jabbok, Peniel ("Face of God"), for he said "I have seen God face to face, and yet my life is preserved."[202] The angelic three visitations to Jacob now Israel conveys the idea that God was building His Kingdom through him and not Esau his twin brother. Indeed, God was with him as He was with Abraham and Isaac in spite of their flaws. In spite of the enormity of the fear that engulfed Israel because of his brother Esau, still the former had to meet with the latter for reconciliation, mutuality and harmony.

"Esau received him kindly, embracing him tearfully with no sign of anger or bitterness."[203] Though the enemy devised his deadly mechanism by influencing Rebekah and Israel (Jacob) to cunningly rob Esau that called for a heavier retaliation from Esau, but God calmed the raging spiritual, emotional, mental, and physical battle. From human point of view Esau should not have received Israel kindheartedly. Rather, Esau should have avenged Jacob instantly and rigorously. After Esau and Jacob's fraternal reunion they parted to their respective destinations in the land of Canaan (Gen. 33:16-20).

Jacob now settled in Shechem in the land of Canaan, bought a piece of land, "built an altar to El-Elohe-Israel (God, the God of Israel). The name of the altar resonates with his encounter with the divine agent who changed his name from Jacob to Israel (Gen. 32:28). "Jacob was thus rendered persona non grata and was commanded by

---

[200] Ibid., 463, 465.

[201] Ibid., 465.

[202] Ibid.

[203] Ibid.

God to go to Bethel."²⁰⁴ Israel obeyed the voice of God and moved to Bethel. Before leaving Jacob wished to purify his camp and took all the "foreign gods" and buried them "under the oak that was near Shechem,"²⁰⁵ a sign of remorse and repentance.

Jacob gave reverence to the God who had mercy on him, kept him safe in Haran, prospered his life, revealed Himself to him, and delivered him from the outrageous anger and death threats of Esau (Gen. 35:1). Cleansing his household was the right approach for continuous grace, mercy, provision, and presence of the God of Abraham and Isaac. Jacob suffered much uncertainty, misery, pain, and sorrow from Genesis chapter 34 and 35, but God was able to reconcile Esau and his brother Isaac. A vivid proof is that when their father Isaac died, his sons Esau and Jacob buried him. (Gen. 35:29).

Israel and the Nations

"Within the Pentateuch, the "children [sons] of Israel" *(bene-yis-ra-el,* usually translated as the gentilic "Israelites") refers generally to the members of the twelve tribes of Israel—as an ethnic designation for the descendants of the eponymous ancestor Israel/Jacob."²⁰⁶ "The sons of Leah; Reuben, Jacob's firstborn, and Simeon, and Levi and Judah, and Issachar, and Zebulon: The sons of Rachel; Joseph, and Benjamin: And the sons of Bilhah, Rachel's handmaid; Gad, and Asher: these are the sons of Jacob, which were born to him in Padan-aram." (Gen. 35:23-26).

The spiritual warfare escalated as Jacobs' ten sons (apart from Benjamin), consumed with rage; conspired together and sold Joseph—"for twenty pieces of silver" (Gen. 37:28). There were three specific reasons for their actions: (1) Israel (Jacob) "loved Joseph more than all his children, because he was the son of his old age" (Gen. 37:3a); (2) The father's love for the son was so intense that "he made him a coat with many colors" (Gen. 37:3b); and (3) The brothers of Joseph envied his dream (Gen. 37:5-11)—"his

---

[204] Ibid., 466.

[205] Ibid.

[206] Robin Knauth, "Israelites," in *Dictionary of Old Testament Pentateuch*, ed. T. Desmond Alexander (Downers Grove: InterVarsity Press, 2003), 452.

outrageous dreams of lordship and supremacy.[207] Joseph's brothers trapped him in the fields just to kill him (Gen. 37:18-25). "Jealousy boils over into violence when the brothers catch Joseph alone in the open country."[208] No one could have saved Joseph apart from the God of Isaac, and Israel (Jacob). God used Judah to save the life of Joseph from being murdered by his brothers (Gen. 37:26).

"Come, and let us sell him to the Ishmaelites, and let not our hand be upon him; for he is our brother and our flesh. And his brethren were content" (Gen. 37:27). Their rage declined a little as Judah spoke those heart penetrating words to them. They agreed with Judah to sell him after they had "striped Joseph out of his coat, his coat of many colors that was on him" (Gen. 37: 23). Finally, they sold their brother Joseph to Midianite merchants (Gen. 37:28). Away with the dreamer, away with the one our father loves most, away with the boy who has a coat with many colors. They wanted to disconnect him from their midst, and even from the land of the living to avoid further heartache as a result of jealousy, envy, bitterness, and anger. In disguise they murdered Joseph—their future savior.

Back from feeding their father's flock in Shechem, they showed the blood soaked coat of their hated brother Joseph. "Is this your son's cloak?"[209] What was Jacob's reaction towards this heart breaking question? The enemy was a work, giving the ten sons ill-invented ideas to appeal to the conscience of their father Jacob who in collaboration with his mother, plotted evil and deceived both Isaac and Esau. "Jacob is devastated on seeing the torn and bloody remnant of the cloak."[210] Thus, "...Jacob rent his clothes, and put sackcloth upon his loins, and mourned for his son many days" (Gen. 37:34). Nothing could stop Jacob from mourning his son for Joseph was dearly loved by his father. Actually, Joseph was not dead, rather he was in Egypt (a foreign land) as a slave sold by his own brothers—the beginning of Israel's exile in an alien land for four centuries to

---

[207] Longacre, "Joseph," 470.

[208] Ibid.

[209] Ibid.,

[210] Ibid.

fulfill the word of God spoken to Abraham on behalf of his children (Gen. 15:13).

"And the LORD was with Joseph, and he was a prosperous man; and he was in the house of his mater the Egyptian" (Gen. 39:2). The dreamer's dream began to unfold in the house of his master Potiphar, "And his mater saw that the LORD was with him, and that the LORD made that he did to prosper in his hand." "There, his virtue, wisdom, and grace quickly established him in leadership."[211] The divine traits demonstrated through Joseph in the house of Potiphar propelled him to excel in leadership qualities, and it served as a floodgate of God's blessing that flooded his master's household in an unprecedented way. At the same time the devil devised a strategy to demoralize Joseph and crush his dream. Thus, the devil's spiritual warfare surfaced alongside Joseph's rise to prominence and favor in Potiphar's house. This time, the enemy worked through the wife of Joseph's master. Burned with excruciating lust (immoral love), Potiphar's wife requested Joseph persistently to have illicit affair with her, but the slave boy Joseph determinedly refused to succumb to that detestable plot of Satan manifested through Potiphar's wife (Gen. 39:7-10).

The selfless devotion of Joseph irritated Potiphar's wife, and she angrily bore false witness against innocent and God-fearing Joseph (Gen. 39:17). Potiphar did not waste time all, but he "put him into prison, a place where the king's prisoners were bound: and he was there in the prison" (Gen. 39:20). "A foreigner, he is maligned and imprisoned"[212] because he feared and revered, the God of his forefathers. Joseph's genuine and intense recognition of God reflects in his pin-point question to his master's wife when she trapped him. Joseph said, "How then can I do this great wickedness, and sin against God?" (Gen. 39:9b). The devil is a liar and he cannot stand the truth; he is embittered and restless whenever he is confronted with biblical truth. He fights against the truth by framing violent and degrading lies to pave his way through. "Joseph's degradation (Gen. 39:7-23), portrays a lively fracas between Potiphar's wife and

---

[211] LaSort, Hubbard, and Bush, *Old Testament Survey*, (Grand Rapids: William B. Eerdmans, 1996), 48.

[212] Ibid.,

Joseph as she tries to persuade him to lie with him."[213] However, God turned Joseph's degradation to an outstanding vindication narrated in the following pages. Faithfulness to, and reverential fear of God accentuates God's miraculous vindication in the midst of traumatic times in spiritual warfare.

"Just as Joseph had gone to the top in Potiphar's estate, he now rises to the position of first trustee in the jail, and everything prospers under his management."[214] Joseph's God-given exceptional leadership skill exploded his vindication in prison. Though the enemy aggressively worked to paralyze the Joseph's dream, the Giver and Fulfiller of Joseph's dreams to advance His Kingdom proved beyond every authority and power to vindicate humble and God-fearing Joseph.

Though still in prison, God used Joseph to interpret dreams of his fellow inmates (Gen. 40). In course of time Pharaoh had similar dreams that bothered him but his magicians and the wise men could not interpret his dreams, and upon a recommendation by a former prison inmate whose dream was interpreted by Joseph but now been released Pharaoh summoned Joseph to come and interpret his dreams (Gen. 41:9-14). God's chosen vessel for this business was Joseph—the dreamer who had been rejected and displaced by his own ten brothers, and the young Hebrew boy who landed in prison because of his unwavering faith and reliance on the God of his forefathers.

At the king's command Joseph was brought from the dungeon—Joseph's horrible domicile (Gen. 41:14). The bushy bearded jail slave wearing shameful prison attire could not appear before Pharaoh with such an appearance. Joseph had to come to the ruler in a decent outfit. On seeing Joseph, Pharaoh implored him to interpret his dreams (Gen. 41:15). Spirit-filled and God-fearing Joseph said, "It is not in me: God shall give Pharaoh an answer of peace" (Gen. 41:16). With humility towards God, and unwavering courage towards Pharaoh Joseph made it clear and straight forward to Pharaoh that he was not the revealer of secrets but the Sovereign

---

[213] Ibid., 471.

[214] Ibid.

King who owns the whole universe and reigns forever would give him the interpretation. Joseph interpreted Pharaoh's two dreams, which had the same meaning (Gen. 41:25-36).

After Joseph had interpreted Pharaoh's dreams the latter said to his servants; "Can we find such a one as this is, a man in whom the Spirit of God is?" (Gen. 41:3). The once slave boy in a foreign land, and a prisoner with false pretenses was appointed second in command by the king of the land where he resided as an alien. The God of Abraham, Isaac, and Jacob subdued all powers and authorities to prove His faithfulness to subjects of His Kingdom and showed Himself all-powerful, all-knowing, all-faithful, and the sovereign King who reigns and rules over all kingdoms and dominions. He worked miraculously to outwit all human and spiritual wisdom, and magical powers to vindicate His humble, faith-filled, uncompromising servant through whom Israel would be delivered from reproach, torture, servitude, rigorous hunger and starvation in Egypt for four centuries, and finally move as a nation to go and posses their inheritance (the promised land).

Joseph's God-given dream was nearing its commencement, but "the promise of land and nationhood must wait to be fulfilled specifically through God's dramatic redemption from slavery in Egypt and the taking of Canaan under Joshua."[215] God's strategy would compel Joseph's father Jacob, his brothers (his betrayers), and their respective households to sojourn to Egypt in search of food to survive the impending famine. The sovereignty of God is revealed in all nations and generations in His redemptive plan for humanity in spite of all impediments; what is required is that; those who have part of His covenant are implored "to live a life of trust and faith in [H]him who calls."[216] Between the time of promise and its fulfillment is when children of God stumble, retreat, break faith, wallow in muddy grounds, fall off, and hastily take decision, among others—a time of testing by God, and a time of tempting by Satan.

Joseph succeeded in his famine-relief program, and all peoples went to him in Egypt to buy grain to survive the famine. In God's

---

[215] LaSort, Hubbard, and Bush, 48.
[216] Ibid., 50.

appointed time Jacob and his household moved to Egypt on the invitation of Pharaoh (Gen. 41:53-45:1-28). "Jacob, his children and all their children excitedly packed their tents and possessions in the wagons and with their flocks, made the long trip to Egypt."[217] As partial fulfillment of His promise the covenant keeping God moved the heart of Pharaoh to painstakingly involve in the evacuation of Jacob and his household from Canaan to Egypt. At Beer-sheba God revealed Himself to Jacob and re-affirmed His active involvement to move them to Egypt, and that he should not entertain any trepidation.

When Jacob and his household arrived in Egypt, "Joseph welcomed his aged father with joyful embraces and tears."[218] What a day in the annals of the Jacob and Joseph? A day of reunion, a day of mixed feeling, a surprising day of humiliation of the enemy, and more importantly a day of celebration of God's faithfulness. God made Jacob and his household favorably disposed toward Pharaoh. The ruler invited them to live in the land of Goshen, a fertile region in the northeast Nile Delta not far from Avaris.[219] Wrights continues that; "it was an excellent grazing area, well suited to the semi nomadic life of the Patriarchal families."[220] The supernatural dominance of God's reign and rule opened a greater door of blessing for Abraham and his descendants. In fulfilling this promise of His the sovereignty of God's power and providence subdued every plan and pretension of His program. "The nation was now there in a germ, and the promises to Abraham were being fulfilled."[221] At the appointed time God began to build the nation Israel in Egypt to fulfill His promise to Abraham in Genesis 15:13.

After the death of Joseph and his brothers "the children of Israel were fruitful, and increased abundantly, and multiplied, and waxed exceedingly mighty; and the land was filled with them" (Exod. 1:7). It is undeniably obvious that the zeal of God made those outstanding

---

[217] G. E. Wright, *Great People of the Bible and How They Lived* (Pleasantville, NY: The Reader's Digest Association Inc., 1979), 67.

[218] Ibid.,

[219] Ibid.

[220] Ibid.

[221] R. E. Longacre "Joseph" in *Dictionary in the Old Testament Pentateuch:* ed.T. Desmond Alexander Downers Grove: InterVarsity Press, 2003) 473.

OLD TESTAMENT ANTECEDENT OF "THE KINGDOM OF GOD"

accomplishments according to His matchless faithfulness and binding promises. God prepared Moses, a Levite to lead his chosen people (Israel) from Egypt to Canaan, the promise land. Wright' insight is noteworthy:

> Jacob had lived in Egypt for nearly four centuries. Most of those years had been good ones. The Israelites had lived peacefully, raising their families and tending their flocks in the fertile Nile delta region the Bible calls Goshen. Then, about 1580 B.C., the native Egyptians revolted against their alien rulers, the Semitic Hyksos who had been friendly to Joseph and his descendants. After destroying The Hyksos capital at Avaris, near Goshen, the Egyptians reunited their country under a native Pharaoh, who ruled from Thebes in Southern Egypt.[222]

In the middle part of the fourth century of Israel's stay in Egypt, there arose a severe spiritual warfare. "There Pharaoh Seti I and his successor, Rameses II—the Pharaoh of Exodus—launched an ambitious building program;"[223] a tedious job that was manually done with strenuous supervision. "But the more they afflicted them, the more they multiplied and grew. And they were grieved because of the children of Israel" (Gen. 1:12). The devil irritated the hearts of the Egyptians against the Hebrew slaves; the Egyptians made the life of the Hebrew slaves very unbearable and uncomfortable.

The hatred of the Egyptians against the Hebrew grew intensely that Pharaoh gave an atrocious command that, "Every son that is born ye shall cast into the river, but every daughter ye shall save alive" (Gen. 1:22). That offensive order of Pharaoh was applicable to only the Hebrew slaves. Egypt did not need any more slave boy to survive and increase the growing number of fighting men who might war against Egypt in the future. In spite of the mistreatment by the Egyptians, the Israelites population grew tremendously. God was

---

[222] Wright, 70.

[223] Ibid.

with His chosen ones working behind the scene to fulfill His promises; "but in God's own time and on God's own terms."[224] God's timing was nearing its fulfillment. The spiritual warfare was severe against the Israelites, and they were subject to ridicule and mockery, but it was a fulfillment of God's word (Gen. 15:13).

After Pharaoh had given that cold-blooded order Moses was born by two Hebrew couple (Gen. 2:1-2); "the man chosen by God to lead the escape from Egypt, to hand down the Law, and shepherd the children of Israel to the gates of the Promised Land."[225] "Moses is mentioned over seven hundred times in the OT (nearly three hundred times in Exodus alone,"[226] "the key figure in the Pentateuchal narratives from Exodus to Deuteronomy... promulgator of the law, organizer of the tribes in work, and worship, and their charismatic leader."[227] The one God foreordained to confront Pharaoh with supernatural power and subdue all the supernatural powers of Egypt, prevail over the powers of other nations on their way to the promise land was born during that period of Israel's severe ill-treatment and annihilation of male born child.

In God's miraculous intervention, Moses was saved from the deadly plot of Pharaoh to kill all Hebrew male born children. That unique deliverance was executed through the daughter of Pharaoh at the bank of the river Nile (Gen. 2:2-6). God moved the heart of Pharaoh's daughter to have extraordinary compassion for the 'poor' Hebrew toddler who was placed along the Nile under the supervision of the toddler's sister who "stood afar off, to wit what would be done to him" (Gen. 2:4). God provided financial support for Moses' mother through Pharaoh's daughter. The name was given by Pharaoh's daughter. "Moses' name is explained in the biblical text by the fact that he was drawn (Heb. *masa*) out of the water."[228] The name Moses "constitutes a wordplay between the Hebrew name

---

[224] LaSort, Hubbard, and Bush, 51.

[225] Wright, 70.

[226] Mark Chavalas, "Moses," in *Dictionary of Old Testament Pentateuch,* ed. T. Desmond Alexander (Downers Grove: InterVarsity Press, 2003), 570.

[227] LaSort, Hubbard, and Bush, 64.

[228] Chavalas, 573.

Moseh and the verb *masa* to draw out.[229] Moses grew in the palace of Pharaoh, and he was raised up by Pharaoh's daughter as her own son.

The maltreatment of Israel escalated. "From dusk to dawn every day, Moses' father and other slaves labored to make bricks to build huge palaces, granaries, walls, gates and temples for the Pharaoh."[230] In the wake of that traumatic time of slavery and torture the God of Abraham, Isaac, and Jacob had an encounter with Moses to go from Midian where he had taken flight back to Egypt to evacuate Israel to the promise land. The appointed time of God to bring His chosen ones from Egypt to Canaan was just at the door step for He had seen the misery, maltreatment, and the treacherous torture of the Hebrew slaves. Though the devil worked tirelessly through the slave masters of Israel, He had a purpose in allowing them to have that agonized experience; just to fulfill His promise to Abraham about the nation Israel through his seed Isaac, and through Jacob and the land of Canaan as their inheritance.

In his encounter with God Moses inquired; "Behold, when I come unto the children of Israel, and shall say unto them, The God of your forefathers has sent me unto you; and they shall say to me, What is his name? What shall I say unto them? (Exod. 3:13). The God of Abraham, Isaac, and Jacob replied Moses by saying; "I AM THAT I AM: and he said, That shalt thou say unto the children of Israel, I AM hath sent me unto you" (Exod. 3:14). " It is important to share Parker's insight on the name Yahweh:

> Yahweh ('the LORD' in AV (KJV), RV, RSV, NIV, following ho kyrios in LXX, Yahweh Sebaoth ('Lord of [heavenly, angelic] hosts'). 'Yahweh' is God's personal name for Himself, by which his people were to invoke him as the Lord who had taken them into covenant with himself in order to do them good. When God first stated this name to Moses at the burning bush, he explained it as meaning 'I am what I am.' or perhaps most accurately 'I will be what I will be.'

---

[229] LaSort, Hubbard, and Bush, 65.
[230] Wright, 70.

> This was a declaration of independent, self-determining existence (Ex. 3:14-15).[231]

Dr. Baker narrates that, Yahweh "is made up of the Hebrew consonants *yhwh,* called the Tetragrammaton, the "four-letter" word par excellence."[232] A unique name revealed to Moses "the most common designation for God in the Pentateuch, and in fact the most common Hebrew noun in the Bible is Yahweh."[233] "Yahweh, the LORD" (Gen. 2:4 and 1,827 additional times in the Pentateuch; 6, 828 times in the OT; cf. *DCH* 4.122-50; Jenni 1997c, 2.523-24)."[234] The frequency of the name Yahweh in the Pentateuch conveys the idea how significant the name is in the redemptive history of Israel from Egypt to Canaan. Moses was called and sent by Yahweh the Great I am to lead the children of Israel from Egypt in the timing, leading, power, and provision of Yahweh—a fulfillment of Yahweh's promise to Abraham (Gen. 15:13-16).

Though Moses persistently objected his calling with many flimsy excuses, he finally concede to Yahweh's calling and proceeded to Egypt with his family (Exod. 3:11-4:1-31). Moses was overwhelmed by human limitations such as; no recognition by the children of Israel, defection in speech, fear of Pharaoh, among others. But his conviction of God's calling was weightier than the spiritual warfare waged against him by the devil through his (Moses) own human thoughts and estimations. At the climax of Yahweh's encounter with Moses, the servant/leader of Yahweh and His chosen people succumb to the extraordinary call of the God of his fathers.

"The first nine plagues are a continuous series (7:8-10:29)."[235] In spite of the stubborn and persistent refusal of Pharaoh to let the people of Yahweh to go out of Egypt to worship Him (Exod. 7:10-10:1-29) the King of all kingdoms proved Himself beyond human

---

[231] J. Parker, "God," in *New Dictionary of Theology,* ed. Sinclair B. Ferguson (Downers Grove: InterVarsity Press, 1988), 274-275.

[232] David Baker, "God, Names of," in *Dictionary of Old Testament Pentateuch,* ed. T. Desmond Alexander (Downers Grove: InterVarsity Press, 2003), 362.

[233] Ibid., 362.

[234] Ibid., 359.

[235] LaSort, Hubbard, and Bush, 68.

and spiritual powers to dominate and subdue Pharaoh's authority and led Israel out of Egypt. "And the LORD said unto Moses, Yet I will bring one plague more upon Pharaoh, and upon Egypt; afterwards he will let you go hence: when he shall let you go, he shall surely thrust you out hence altogether" (Exod. 11:1). Nevertheless, Yahweh had a divine timing to get His people out of Egypt to outwit all opposing powers (both spiritual and physical).

Yahweh gave specific command to Moses to pass onto the children of Israel prior to their exit from Egypt (Exod. 11:2-110). "For I will pass through the land of Egypt this night, and will smite all the firstborn in the land of Egypt, both man and beast; and against all the gods of Egypt I will execute judgment: I am the LORD" (Exod. 12:12). Every household of the children of Israel was asked to kill an unblemished little lamb and use the blood to mark the door posts of their respective houses, remain in, with specific food items (Exod. 12:1-11). "And the blood shall be to you a token upon the houses where ye are: and when I see the blood, I will pass over you, and the plague shall not be upon you to destroy you, when I smite the land of Egypt" (Exod. 12:13). Yahweh was about to pour His wrath on Pharaoh and the land of Egypt to hasten the exit of Israel from servitude of Pharaoh and Egypt.

Yahweh foreknew the day and hour that Pharaoh would surrender to the mandated authority of Moses. When the plague struck that night, death came to every house in Egypt; beginning from Pharaoh to ordinary Egyptian. Yahweh's sovereign rule and reign over all creation, kingdoms, dominions, powers, spirits, and authorities surfaced when He executed judgment on all first born of Israel's slave masters. Consumed with outrageous tremble, and sorrow mixed with anger Pharaoh could not show any resistance again than to plead with Aaron and Moses to go with Israel and all their belongings to worship the Lord. It very funny Pharaoh requested Aaron and Moses to bless him (Exod. 12:32).

At the appointed time Yahweh fulfilled His promise to Abraham to evacuate his descendants from the land of slavery to a spacious land flowing with milk and honey. (Gen. 15:13-14). "In great haste, Moses and his people gathered up their belongings and began their flight from Egypt to Canaan, the Promised Land."[236] "And the children of Israel journeyed from Rameses to Succoth, about six hundred thousand on foot that were men, beside children"(Exod. 12:37). Chavalas advocates that; "The Bible portrays the Israelites as having left Pi-Ramesse, moving in a southeastern direction toward the Tjeku region."[237] "And Moses took the bones of Joseph with him, for he had strictly sworn the children of Israel, saying, God will surely visit you; and ye shall carry up my bones away hence with you" (Exod. 13:19). Moses was very careful to remember Joseph through whom Yahweh saved Jacob and his descendants from starving to death.

"And the LORD went before them by day in a pillar of a cloud, to lead them the way; and by night in a pillar of fire, to give them light; to go by day and night" (Exod. 13:21). The devil intensified spiritual warfare through Pharaoh against the children of Israel. Pharaoh was dissatisfied for allowing Israel to leave Egypt as their slaves. Again, Yahweh hardened "Pharaoh's heart, that he shall follow after them; and I will be honored upon Pharaoh, and upon all his host; that the Egyptians may know that I am the LORD" (Exod. 14:4). Pharaoh broke his promise and sent a contingent of charioteers to capture them.[238] The horsemen and their chariots chased the children of Israel to the shore of the Red Sea (Exod. 14:3-9).

Seeing the Egyptians, Israel was thrown into a great panic. They cried to God and at the same time accused Moses for "seemingly" raising their hopes like a vapor (Exod. 14:10-12). Moses the servant of God said to the children of Israel, "Fear ye not, stand still, and see the salvation of the LORD, which he will show to you today: for the Egyptians whom ye have seen today, ye shall see them again no more forever" (Exod.14:13). Moses further said, "The LORD shall fight for you, and ye shall hold your peace" (Exod. 14:14). Thus, the I AM who began the miraculous deliverance to fulfill His promise will complete it.

"And the children of Israel went into the midst of the sea upon the dry ground: and the waters were a wall unto them on their right hand,

---

[236] Wright, 78.

[237] Chavalas, 575.

[238] Wright, 79.

and on their left" (Exod. 14:22). Fretheim adds that; "The people were finally delivered when God parted the waters of the Red Sea for the Israelites to pass through but closed them up again to engulf the pursuing Egyptians."[239] Though Pharaoh proved very stubborn Yahweh proved His omnipotence over both the powers of the devil and that of Pharaoh. The intensified spiritual warfare had come to its fulfillment with the furious assailants of the children of Israel drown in the Red Sea. None of them survived. Satanic agents and forces could not stand the Yahweh who rules and reigns creation as the Creator God.

Moses and Israel burst into an atmosphere of spontaneous and ceaseless praise and worship to Yahweh. "Then sang Moses and the children of Israel this song unto the LORD, and spake, saying, I will sing unto the LORD, for he hath triumphed gloriously: the horse and his rider hath he thrown into the sea" (Exod. 15:1). Moses as well as his sister Miriam offered songs of adoration, exaltation, deliverance, and thankfulness to the God of Abraham, Isaac, and Jacob (Exod. 15:2-21).

Surprising to the Israelites, a band of armed men aggressively confronted them. How did Israel fight this battle? From human point of view Israel was no match to the Amalekites in terms of experience and weapons. A spiritual warfare waged by the evil one and being made manifest in the flesh, from all indications Israel was naïve and fragile, but Yahweh routed Amalekites through a unique divine strategy (Exod. 17:8-13). After God had miraculously given Israel victory Moses he "built an altar, and called the name of it Jehovah-nissi" (Exod. 17:15) for the Lord is their Defense, Victory, and Banner.

"In the third month, when the children of Israel were gone forth out of the land of Egypt, the same day came they into the wilderness of Sinai" (Exod. 19:1). A writer says:

> On arriving at Mt. Sinai, the people camped before the mountain. Moses ascended the mountain to meet

---

[239] Terrence Fretheim, "Exodus, Book Of," in *Dictionary of Old Testament Pentateuch*, ed. T. Desmond Alexander (Downers Grove: InterVarsity Press, 2003), 249.

with God. There God informed him that he was going to enter into a covenant with Israel that they might become God's own possession among all peoples. The condition was "if you obey my voice and keep my covenant" (19:5). In a three day period of consecration the people were to wash their clothes and make themselves and make themselves ready (vv. 9-15). At the foot of the mountain (v. 17), the momentous event began. God manifested himself in awe-inspiring majesty:[240]

Yahweh visited Israel at Mt. Sinai to formally have a covenant with them that would accentuate theocratic rule over them as His possession among all peoples of the earth. In the midst of these strange and scary moments Yahweh summoned Moses and delivered the Ten Commandments (Exod. 20:1-17). Yahweh began by saying, "I am the LORD thy God, which have brought thee out of the land of Egypt, out of the house of bondage" (Exod. 20:2). Yahweh warned Israel that; "Thou shalt have no other gods before me" (Exod. 20: 3). Israel trembled and implored Moses to speak with them instead of Yahweh (Exod. 20:19). However, Moses cautioned the children of Israel, "Fear not: for God is come to prove you, and that his fear may be before your faces, that ye sin not" (Exod. 20:20). LaSort narrates that:

> For thirty-eight years after they had balked at entering Canaan, the Israelites were restrained in the wilderness of Paran and at Kadesh-barnea. Only when the generation had died off, were they permitted to resume their journey. God led them in a long detour up the east side of Edom. Then they were ordered to camp Moab, awaiting final instructions to cross the Jordan river and possess the promised land."[241]

---

[240] LaSort, Hubbard, and Bush, 72.
[241] Ibid., 111.

Though Yahweh in diverse ways defended and delivered Israel from opposing powers, the spiritual warfare continued in the wilderness as Satan lured Israel to worship idols as the nations. Israel disobeyed disbelieved, grumbled, murmured among other demonic traits against Yahweh. Hence, the acts of Israel crippled the generation who left Egypt to the land of Canaan with the exception of Joshua and Caleb who grew firmly in their faith and faithfulness to Yahweh. Israel's rebellion escalated day after day. Yahweh was displeased with gross insubordination to His word and directions. Caleb and Joshua proved themselves right in the sight of Yahweh. Joshua continued from where Moses ended and led Israel to the Promised Land and shared the land to the tribes of Israel under the instructions and supervision of Yahweh.

The successor of Moses "was "Hoshea" ("salvation," cf. Num. 13:8), but Moses called him "Jehoshua" or "Joshua" ("Yahweh is salvation"; v. 16)."[242] Moses' aide Joshua (Greek, *Jesous* "Jesus") was chosen by Moses to be his "minister"—probably his personal attendant (NRSV. "assistant")—and was present on the mountain when Moses received the law (Exod. 24:13ff.)."[243] Yahweh prepared Joshua for the task; "he experienced the deliverance from Egypt, the giving of the law at Sinai, the terrible frustrations and sufferings of the wilderness, and the tremendous leadership of Moses."[244] Yahweh promised His new servant (Joshua) that everywhere his foot "shall tread," it would be given unto him (Josh. 1:3).

After leading His people to cross over the Jordan River Yahweh commanded Joshua to instruct all males among Israel to circumcise before the fall of Jericho wall (Josh. 3-5). The covenant keeping God wanted the descendants of Abraham to stick to that sign of circumcision to fulfill His spoken word. After the males among the children of Israel were circumcised at Gilgal, Yahweh appeared to Joshua. Seeing a strange man with a sword courageous Joshua approached that Divine Agent and inquired his mission. During the cradle of the call of Joshua Yahweh cautioned Him to be strong and courageous

---

[242] Ibid., 142.

[243] Ibid.

[244] Ibid., 143.

(Josh. 1: 6, 7, 9), so Joshua demonstrated his courage and strength in Yahweh. A man of God leading the people of God amidst many opposing powers and authorities had to be a man of courage and strength in the One who called him and gave him that unique assignment in the Mission of God, *missio Dei* (Josh. 5:13-15).

Unfortunately for Jericho their aggressive defense strategy failed as Yahweh chose a strategy that is beyond human mind to comprehend. Joshua's unwavering obedience sealed the divine approach with outstanding victory. Rahab who is found in the genealogy of Jesus Christ (Matt. 1:5) was spared because of her distinguished faith in the God of the Hebrews and His mission (Josh.6:22-25). Israel had a reason to celebrate their overwhelming victory over fortified city Jericho and its inhabitants.

In the leading and power of Yahweh Joshua and the children of Israel triumphed over many nations and kings (Josh. 12:7-24).

Yahweh's promise to Abraham to give the allotted to his descendants came to fruition in spite of the magnitude of spiritual warfare waged by Satan through spiritual beings, and various kings of nations. Joshua chapters 13 through 21:42 narrate the sharing of the land flowing with honey and milk to the children of Israel according to their tribes. Subjects of the Kingdom of God have an unflinching assurance of His faithfulness with the condition of undaunted obedience to, and resolute faith in the covenant keeping God. From the time of the promise of the land to the time of possessing the land was almost five centuries, but "...the LORD gave unto Israel all the land which he sware to give unto their fathers; and they possessed it, and dwelt therein" (Josh. 21:43).

In the course of time when Israel was at the mercy of the Philistines, Yahweh rejected Saul as the king of Israel because of his disobedience to the word of God (I Sam. 12-15). The spiritual warfare escalated amidst intimidation pressure, mockery, among other ugly insinuations. That called for a new king of Israel who would obey Yahweh. Yahweh sent Samuel to go to the house of Jesse and anoint one of his sons He (Yahweh) had chosen to be king (I Sam. 16:1b). Though David was the youngest among his brothers, he was the one Yahweh chose to lead his people Israel (I Sam. 16:6-12). Was that the first time Yahweh chose younger brother over the elder? No, it was not. Similar incidents include "Isaac over Ishmael, Jacob over Esau, Joseph over the ten brothers,"[245] and David over his bothers. Again LaSort posits that, "This pattern highlights these events as turning points in God's redemptive program."[246] The sovereignty of Yahweh transcends estimations and choices, cultures, traditions, among other human limitations. A champion in the Philistine army named Goliath rained insults on Israel for almost forty days (I Sam. 17:1-16). Dr. McGee says "The men of Israel cringed in cowardly fashion at the boasting and braggadocio of this man."[247] Saul and his army were paralyzed with fear and hopelessness as the Philistine's giant physically, emotionally, mentally, and psychologically tortured them with words and his unusual physique. Yahweh caused young David (His anointed king) to slay the Philistine giant, Goliath, in a miraculous way (I Sam. 17:40-58). David's words were actualized by Yahweh (I Sam. 17:45).

The courage and the bravery David exercised in his counter-utterance with the over nine feet tall Goliath (I Sam. 17:4), was under the impulse of the Spirit of God. "David stood before this massive creature unintimidated"[248] and said, "This day will the LORD deliver thee into mine hand; and I will smite thee, and take thine head from thee; and I will give the carcasses of the host of the Philistines this day unto the fowls of the air, and to the wild beasts of the earth; that all the earth may know that there is a God in Israel" (I Sam. 17:46).

"Out of this battle, the real truth emerged, evident to the troops on both sides of the Valley of Elah: Goliath was the dwarf and David was the giant."[249] After David had killed Goliath and cut off his head the Philistines ran for their dear lives as the men of Israel gave them a severe chase and took their spoils (I Sam. 17:49-52). That great accomplishment of David, the servant of God brought a great relief of distress, fear, intimidation, and mockery, for the people of

---

[245] LaSort, Hubbard, and Bush, 176.

[246] Ibid.

[247] J. Vernon McGee, *David: A Man After God's Own Heart* (Nashville, TN: Thomas Nelson Publishers, 2000), 4.

[248] Charles Swindoll, *David: A Man of Passion and Destiny* (Nashville, TN: W. Publishing Group, 1997), 46.

[249] Ibid., 47.

God. Though Satan used Israel's perennial and perpetual enemy, the Philistines[250] on many occasions to attack Israel, Yahweh gave successive victories to Israel through the leadership of David. (2 Sam. 5: 17-25; 8:1-14; 21:15-22).

With the guidance and help of Yahweh David subdued the enemies of Israel and made Jerusalem a fortified city of David. Yahweh was the divine Agent behind the overwhelming triumph of the former shepherd boy called by Yahweh to be the king of His people. The covenanted people of God enjoyed peace under the kingship of David. King David recognized that Yahweh was the Source of his sufficiency, so as a token of his love and appreciation to Him one of the king's main worry was where the ark of the covenant of God was placed (II Sam. 7:1-2). Yahweh recognized the genuine outflow of the heart of His servant David; a heart of worship and praise to the King of all kings.

Yahweh sent His prophet Nathan to David with this message:

> And when thy days be fulfilled, and thou shalt sleep with thy fathers, I will set up thy seed after thee, which shall proceed out of thy bowels, and I will establish his kingdom. He shall build a house for my name, and I will establish the throne of his kingdom forever. I will be his father, and he shall be my son. If he commits iniquity, I will chasten him with the rod of men, and with the stripes of the children of men. But my mercy shall not depart away from him, as I took it Saul, whom I put away before thee. And thine house and thine kingdom shall be established forever before thee: thy throne should be established forever. According to all these words, and according to all this vision, did Nathan speak unto David. (2 Sam. 7:12-17)

When David heard the word of Yahweh through the prophet Nathan David burst out to praise the God of Abraham, Isaac,

---

[250] McGee, 1.

and Jacob. A shepherd boy from the tribe of Judah, an unpopular country boy, the least among the sons of Jesse, an outcast by his own brothers, a murderer and an adulterer, among others, Why should Yahweh have such an unmerited favor for me by promising me an everlasting kingdom? Well...Yahweh chose to do that without any constraints for His own glory (II Sam. 7:18).

In fulfillment of the promise of Yahweh King Solomon the son of David, built a house for the name of Yahweh and "Now when Solomon had made an end of praying, the fire came down from heaven, and consumed the burnt offering and the sacrifices; and the glory of the LORD filled the house" (2 Chron. 7:1).

Yahweh promised to hearken to the prayers that are said in the house built by Solomon. Yahweh required the people who are called by His matchless name to approach Him with hearts of penitence and humility, genuine repentance and remorse, and seek Him with diligence. Yahweh promised relief, restoration, healing and Godly satisfaction to the children of Israel in return to the unadulterated obedience to His command (II Sam. 7:12-15). The other part of Yahweh's promise to David to give him an everlasting house, throne, and kingdom was realized through Jesus Christ the son of David (Mark 10:47), and the Son of God (Luke 1:35; John 3:16). This would be discussed in the next chapter.

CHAPTER 5

"THE KINGDOM OF GOD" IS SPIRITUAL WARFARE IN THE NEW TESTAMENT

John the Baptist

"As it was written in the prophets, Behold, I send my messenger before thy face, which shall prepare thy way before thee" (Mark. 1:2). This fulfilled the prophecy, "The voice of him that crieth in the wilderness Prepare ye the way of the LORD, make straight in the desert a highway for our LORD" (Isa. 40:3). Who is that messenger of God? The messenger was "John the Baptist or John the Baptizer,"[251] a "wonder-child."[252] The mother of John the Baptist was Elizabeth (Luke 1:40-57), and his father was Zacharias (Luke 1:67). The writer of the Gospel of Mathew provides a vivid description of John: "…John had his raiment of camel's hair, and a leather girdle about his loins; and his meat was locusts and wild honey" (Matt. 3:4)." Dr. Ben Witherington III advocates, "Luke alone informs us that John was born into a pious and priestly family, to parents well advanced in age."[253] He further advocates that, "All

---

[251] Ben Witherington III, "John the Baptist," in *Dictionary of Jesus and the Gospels*, ed. Joel B. Green (Downers Grove: InterVarsity Press, 1992), 383.

[252] F. F. Bruce, *New Testament History* (New York, NY: Doubleday, 1971), 153.

[253] Witherington, 384

four Gospels associate John with, or treat him as, the "beginning of the gospel."'[254] The frequency of John the Baptist in all the four Gospels confirms the significant role he played as a messenger of God to preach the kingdom of God.

"Now when all the people were baptized, it came to pass, that Jesus also being baptized, and praying, the heaven was opened. And the Holy Ghost descended in a bodily shape like a dove upon him, and a voice came from heaven, which said, Thou art my beloved Son; in thee I am well pleased" (Luke 3: 21-22). John the Baptist came to turn the hearts of Israel to Yahweh, and to introduce the Son of God whom the prophet Isaiah spoke about (Isa. 9:6-7). From the lips of John the Baptist, the One who sent him gave him the clue that the one whom the Holy Ghost would descend upon would be the Son of God. John confirmed Jesus as the One that the Holy Ghost descended upon when he baptized Him in the Jordan River. Bruce argues that from the New Testament writers' point of view, "the climax of John's ministry was his baptism of Jesus."[255] With that convincing proof of Jesus as the Son of the God, the genuine testimony of John the Baptist is valid in the eyes of God and those who fear God.

John's preaching was very offensive to Satan and his allies, the children of Israel, especially the political and religious leaders. Therefore the devil waged a very aggressive war against the messenger and the message of God. Satan is always uncomfortable with the divine truth. He cannot stand it. It uncovers his intentions and works. Satan resolved to stop John the Baptist's unwelcome ministry by killing him. Satan, the murderer dominated the hearts and mind of Herod and his illegitimate wife Herodias to carry out the deed. "But Herod the tetrarch, being reproved by him for Herodias his brother Philip's wife, and for all the evils which Herod had done, added yet above all, that he shut up John in prison" (Luke 3:19-20). John the Baptist frowned at the inappropriate marital life of Herod and Herodias (John 6:18).

---

[254] Ibid., 383.
[255] Bruce, 158.

Finally, on the birthday of Herod, his wife Herodias conspired with her daughter to have John the Baptist killed (Mark 6:21-29). "Both Josephus and the Gospel tradition agree that John lost his life at the hands of Herod Antipas, the ruler of Galilee and Perea."[256] In the eyes of Jesus, John's ministry marked the end of the era of the law and the prophets. "The new era of the kingdom of God followed on the threshold on which John stood as the last and greatest in the long succession of those who foresaw and foretold its advent (Luke 16:16)."[257] Thus, John the Baptist was the last prophet of the Old Testament who spoke of the coming of the new covenant through Jesus Christ. Though John the Baptist was martyred, he accomplished a great ministry in the kingdom of God by drawing the attention of Israel from Abraham to Yahweh, and revealing Jesus Christ as the Son of God to the children of Israel.

Jesus Christ

Who is Jesus Christ? John the Baptist attests that Jesus Christ is the Son of God (John 1:34), "arguably the most significant Christological title in the NT. "Son of God" or its equivalents ("the Son," "my Son," etc.) occur more than 124 times in the NT."[258] "The Son of God "carries a variety of meanings, including commission to special work, obedience, intimate fellowship, knowledge, likeness and the receiving of blessing and gifts.[259] During the divine visitation of the angel Gabriel to the Virgin Mary espoused to Joseph (Luke 1: 26-34), the angel spoke about "the Son of God," "And the angel answered and said unto her, The Holy Ghost shall come upon thee, and the power of the Highest shall overshadow thee: therefore also that holy thing which shall be born of thee shall be called the Son of God" (Luke 1:35).

The title takes us back to his eternal being (Jn. 1:18 NIV), but it is especially the descriptive term of his incarnate life seen as expressing

---

[256] Witherington, 388.

[257] Bruce, *New Testament History*, 162.

[258] David Bauer, "Son of God," in *Dictionary of Jesus and the Gospels*, ed. Joel B. Green (Downers Grove: InterVarsity Press, 1996), 769.

[259] Ibid., 770.

a deep final union from his baptism as the elect one (Mk. 1: 11 par.) onwards."[260] During His baptism, a voice from heaven said; "This is my beloved Son in whom I am well pleased" (Matt. 3:17). Also, on a mountain with Peter, James, and John (Matt. 17:1-4), a voice from Heaven spoke again saying; "This is my beloved Son, in whom I am well pleased, hear ye him" (Matt. 17:5). In these two events, the Father in Heaven attested Jesus Christ as His beloved Son.

Jesus Christ is also designated as "the Son of Man" to fulfill Yahweh's promise to King David—"And, behold, thou shalt conceive in thy womb, and bring forth a son, and shalt call his name JESUS. He shall be great, and shall be called the Son of the Highest: and the Lord God shall give unto him the throne of his father David: And he shall reign over the house of Jacob forever; and of his kingdom there shall be no end" (Luke 1:31-33). "The phrase "the Son of Man" (*ho huios tou anthropou*) is such a form of words. It is the phrase used more frequently than any other (except "Jesus" itself) to refer to Jesus in the Gospels."[261] "The Son of Man" is the "title for Christ, Messiah (Gr. *Huios tou anthropou;* Aram. *bar nasa;* Heb. *ben adam)*."[262] Yahweh spoke to David through the prophet Nathan: "And thine house and thy kingdom shall be established forever before thee: thy throne shall be established forever" (2 Sam. 7: 16). As a man, Jesus Christ belongs to the lineage of David (Matt. 1:1-17; Luke 3:23-31)—the King of all kings who reigns eternally.

Jesus Christ is the "Son of David" (Mark 10:46). Dr. David Bauer posits:When used in christological title, Son of David points to Jesus as royal Messiah

> (see Christ) in the line of David. As such he fulfills the promises God made to David regarding the eternal reign of David's "offspring" (e.g., 2 Sam. 7:12-16),and he acts as the unique agent in bringing

---

[260] R. Martin, "Sonship," in *New Dictionary of Theology,* ed. Sinclair B. Ferguson (Downers Grove: InterVarsity Press, 1988), 653.

[261] Howard Marshall, "Son of Man," in *Dictionary of Jesus and the Gospels,* ed. Joel B. Green (Downers Grove: InterVarsity Press, 1992), 775.

[262] Royce Gruenler, "Son of Man," in *Evangelical Dictionary of Theology* (Grand Rapids: Baker Books, 1984), 1034.

the rule of God (see Kingdom of God) to the earth, a rule that is characterized by salvation and blessing. In contrast to major streams of popular messianic expectations, Jesus refused to establish his kingly rule through political ascendancy or military conquest (see Revolutionary Movements). Rather, this Davidic king wielded his royal power by attending to the needs of the poor and oppressed, and by suffering and dying in order to bring salvation to his people.[263]

Jesus Christ as the son of David was the promised king to inaugurate the kingdom of God and reign as King forever (Eph. 5:5). Unlike earthly kings whose rule is temporal and intimidating, and full of political struggles, the son of David (Jesus) demonstrates His kingly rule by delivering, healing, and saving the lost (oppressed and outcast).

"Jesus' first public appearance was at his baptism in the river Jordan, an event which is commonly, and rightly, regarded as marking the beginning of his ministry."[264] Jesus went from Galilee to John the Baptist at the River Jordan to be baptized (Matt. 3:13-17). Jesus submitted willingly to John's baptism—not because He needed to repent of any sin of his own "for he knew no sin" (2 Cor. 5:21); but as He said, His submission was to "fulfill all righteousness" (Matt. 3:15).

Satan waged war against Jesus Christ after His baptism—termed as "the temptation in the wilderness."[265] "Jesus, the Son of God, meets the Devil, Satan and the tempter, face-to-face in true mortal combat."[266] "The first three Evangelists agree that the Spirit (see Holy Spirit) led Jesus into the wilderness and that he was tempted by Satan (Mk. 1:13) or the devil (Mt. 4:1 par. Lk. 4:2)."[267] What is temptation? In this context, temptation "refers to an attempt, often

---

[263] Bauer, 766-767.

[264] Ibid., 167.

[265] Twelftree, "Temptation of Jesus," 822.

[266] Murphy, 263.

[267] Twelftree, 822.

by Satan (see Demon, Devil, Satan), to incite a person to sin."[268] "Then was Jesus led up of the Spirit into the wilderness to be tempted of the devil. And when he had fasted forty days and forty nights, he was afterward hungry. And when the tempter came to him, he said; if thou be the Son of God, command that these stones be made bread" (Matt. 4:1-3).

Tempting Jesus as the Son of God with the pretense to satisfy His hunger by turning stones into bread Twelftree argues, "This could be seen as a temptation to repeat the miracle (see Miracles and Miracle stories) of the provision of manna in the wilderness (Ex. 16:13-21; 2 Apoc. Bar. 29:1-30:1."[269] Fasting for forty days, certainly Jesus Christ was hungry, so Satan had a seemingly good point to use this to tempt Jesus Christ. Nevertheless, Jesus answered, "It is written, Man shall not live by bread alone, but by every word that proceedeth out of the mouth of God" (Matt. 4:4). Clearly, the words of Jesus convey the idea that He was "satisfied with His Father's nourishment and care"[270] — the spoken Word of God. Yes, Jesus is the Son of God, but He did not want to assert His independence from God the Father.

Asking Jesus Christ to throw himself from a pinnacle just to be rescued by the angels as a fulfillment of God's promise was a misrepresentation and misapplication of Scripture by the devil (Matt. 4:5-6). In contrast to the first temptation appealing to Jesus' physical needs, the second tempted Him towards religious fanaticism."[271] "Jesus said unto him, it is written again, Thou shalt not tempt the Lord thy God" (Matt. 4:7). Jesus rebuked Satan that; it is not right for a creature to tempt his Creator — gross insubordination of Satan.

"In the third temptation, Satan lays aside the subtle approach he used in the first two. Now, in desperation, he throws all caution to the wind. He is losing ground. Frantic to succeed, he comes to the heart of the matter. Satan wants Jesus to pay him homage, tribute,

---

[268] Ibid., 821.

[269] Ibid., 823.

[270] Twelftree, 823.

[271] Murphy, 267.

honor, and service, if only for a moment (Matt. 4:9)."[272] Twelftree suggests; "This final temptation is then, the most devilish of all; the call to Jesus to receive his proper inheritance without obedient worship of God."[273] Jesus answered with a piercing command; "Get thee hence, Satan: for it is written, Thou shalt worship the Lord thy God, and him only shalt thou serve" (Matt. 4:10). Dr. Murphy records that, "Jesus concludes His dismissal of Satan and His word of total commitment to God and His worship, homage, and service."[274] With a sharp rebuke, Jesus put Satan to flight, and finally instructs him to give worship to God who is worthy to be worshipped. In conclusion to the temptation in the wilderness, though Satan waged the war, he was fatally defeated. "Having met the test of the temptations, Jesus is now ready to enter into His proclamation, healing, and deliverance ministry,"[275] in the midst of intense spiritual warfare waged by the arch enemy Satan throughout His unique ministry as "the Son of God", "the Son of Man", and the "son of David."

"Now after that John was put into prison, Jesus came into Galilee, preaching the gospel of the kingdom of God. And saying, [t]The time is fulfilled, and the kingdom of God is at hand: repent ye, and believe the gospel" (Mark 1:14-15).

Robert Guelich asserts that;

> "Jesus ministry has to do with the inauguration of God's sovereign, redemptive rule, the kingdom of God, in history. The exorcisms of the demonic (e.g., 1:21-27), Healing of the sick (e.g., 2:1-12; see Healing), fellowship with sinners (2:13-17), feeding the hungry (e.g., 6:34-44), even the programmatic calling of the Twelve (3:13-19), all give expressions in Mark's story to Jesus' preaching of the "gospel of God, the time has been fulfilled, the kingdom of God

---

[272] Ibid.
[273] Twelftree, 825.
[274] Murphy, 268.
[275] Ibid., 269.

has come ..." as found in the programmatic summary of Jesus' ministry in 1:14-15).[276]

As discussed earlier in Chapter 3, "The Nature of Spiritual warfare," Jesus came to preach, inaugurate, and reveal the kingdom of God to Israel, and humanity as a whole.

Caragounis insists that;

The present activity of the Son of man, especially his casting out of demons, is an integral part of the proclamation of the kingdom of God, but it shall be seen not so much as indicating the actual occurrence of the decisive event of the kingdom of God but as the preliminary warfare of the Son of man against the evil powers in his work of making possible the entrance of the kingdom of God in human history.[277]

The Son of God came to destroy the works of the devil (I John 3:8) in the life of wayward humanity, so that He might deliver humanity from the domain and grips of the devil. In His encounter with Zachaeus, Jesus said, "For the Son of man is come "to seek and to save that which are lost" (Luke 19:10), but I posit that first the devil needs to be subdued by the matchless power of the Holy Spirit before his captives are delivered from the dominion and servitude of the devil, and finally their genuine commitment and sincere surrender to the Son of God.

After raising Lazarus from the dead, the Pharisees and the scribes were outraged as they plotted to kill Jesus Christ (John 11:47-53). The act of kindness extended by Jesus Christ to Lazarus and his family members, and even his community should not have triggered such indignation by the Pharisees and the chief priests that led to their convening a meeting to plot the death of Christ. Jesus Christ, who is; "the resurrection and the life" (John 11:25), subdued

---

[276] Guelich, "Mark, Gospel of," in *The Dictionary of Jesus and the Gospels* ed. Joel B. Green (Downer Grove: InterVarsity Press, 1992), 518.

[277] Caragounis, 425.

death by raising Lazarus back to life—an infringement on the power of and authority of Satan and his demonic forces. The instant prophetic word of Caiaphas was welcomed and the death of Jesus was approved by the Jewish Council (the Sanhedrin) (John 11:53). Thus, Jesus was placed on a wanted list by his antagonistic opponents— intense spiritual warfare was initiated and led by Satan through the Sanhedrin (John 11:56-57).

"This warfare, the Son of man's attacks on the kingdom of evil, ought not to be construed in terms of Hellenistic or Jewish exorcist's activity but rather ought to be connected with the Son of man's mission to 'serve and to give his life a ransom for many' (Mk 10:45 par.); otherwise the link between the kingdom of God and the cross becomes illegitimately obscured."[278] At the right time Jesus had to lay down His life and take it back on behalf of sinful humanity (Rom. 5:6-8)—a vivid demonstration of the matchless love of God for humanity.

According to Mark the Gospel writer, Jesus Christ on three occasions predicted His death and resurrection on the third day (Mark 8:31; 9:31; 10:33-34). "The Lamb of God which takes away the sin of the world" (John 1:29) had to triumph over Satan, death, and sin (Col. 2:15) in order to extend forgiveness to, and impute righteousness upon all those who accept Him into their lives as personal Lord and Savior (Rom. 10:9-10). Jesus had to accomplish His mission partially by His atonement—a selfless sacrifice.

Preparing His disciples to preach the kingdom of God, Jesus chose twelve among them; "[H]he gave them power against unclean spirits, to cast them out, and to heal all manner of sicknesses and all manner of diseases" (Matt. 10:1). The kingdom of God is a power encounter, it is spiritual warfare. It is more than casting out demons and healing the sick among other signs and wonders–though they should not be underestimated as outmoded practices of the kingdom of God. The sick need healing, and the demon-possessed need deliverance from wicked spirits, powers, and authorities. Jesus cautioned His disciples to minister to the needs of others without demanding anything in return (Matt. 10:7-8).

---

[278] Caragounis, 425.

In another development Jesus chose seventy, and sent them to go and preach the kingdom of God (Luke 10:1-16). "And the seventy returned again with joy, saying Lord, even the devils are subject unto us through your name" (Luke 10:17). Again, Jesus emphasized that subjection of Satan and his forces at the mention of His name is established, but they should not be startled; rather, their joy must be complete as children of God—subjects of the kingdom of God (Luke 10:18-20).

Jesus drew the attention of His disciples of the coming of the Holy Spirit. "But when the Comforter is come, whom I will send unto you from the Father, even the Spirit of truth which proceedeth from the Father, he shall testify of me. And ye also bear witness, because ye have been with me from the beginning" (John 15:26-27). The Father in heaven sends the Spirit of truth to bear witness of "the way, the truth, and the life" (John 14:6) in a world dominated by "[the]a liar, and the father of it" (John 8:44). "A divine person, whose dwelling place from all eternity has been at the Father's side, has been sent by Christ to earth to bear witness to [H]him, to be [H]his representative, to be as it were, [H]his other self."[279] The disciples of Jesus Christ also testified of Him because of their active involvement in His ministry, but the witness of the Holy Spirit energized and equipped them with supernatural traits to champion the cause of God (John 16:7-12).

Jesus perceived that in their minds they preferred Him to be with them as rather than another Comforter that Jesus talked about. "They were not able to grasp the significance of the replacement of a limited bodily presence with an unlimited universal presence."[280] The Son of man, (Jesus) was limited to space and time during His ministry in Galilee. It was therefore necessary for the coming of the Holy Spirit. The Holy Spirit would uncover the works of the devil in the lives of humanity, reprimand them, convict them of their sinfulness, and draw their attention to God's judgment that waits for the unrepentant ones.

---

[279] John Phillips, 298.
[280] Ibid., 302.

Jesus taught on the revealing ministry of the Holy Spirit (John 16:13-16). The Holy Spirit's ministry pre-eminently embraces the things of Jesus Christ, and exalts Him as well. "The Lord Jesus had been a living exegesis of the Father; now the Spirit was to be a living exegesis of the Son; all that the Son was would be interpreted by the Spirit."[281] The Son came to reveal the Father (John 1:18); now is the turn for the Holy Spirit to reveal the Son who is one with the Father (John 10:30). Jesus was going to His Father after His bodily death and resurrection on the mount of Calvary.

The appointed time for "the Son of God", "the Son of Man", the "son of David", Jesus Christ to pay the penalty of humanity by death on the cross was near; not because of His own sin, but because of the sin of humanity—a demonstration of God's incomparable love (John 3:16; Rom. 5:6-8). After His agonized intercessory prayer (John 17), "He went forth with his disciples over to the brook Cedron, where was a garden into the which he entered, and his disciples. And Judas, also which betrayed him, knew the place: for Jesus oftentimes resorted thither with his disciples" (John 18:1-2). "So later that evening Jesus and the disciples went to the garden called Gethsemane on the Mount of Olives , and Judas' plan went into operation (Mt. 26:36-56; Mk. 14:26-50; Lk. 22:39-53; Jn. 18:1-14)."[282] The Jewish Council in collaboration with Judas murdered Jesus Christ to satisfy their deep seated hatred (John 18:3).

When Jesus was brought before Pilate he could not find any grounds to convict him, and further instructed the persecutors of Jesus to judge Him according to their law (John 18:29-31a). In talking about His Kingdom, Jesus said; that warranted His coming to earth to testify to that truth about the Kingdom. Pilate was confused again as he asked Jesus about the truth. Convincingly, Pilate found no grounds to approve the hearts' desire of the Jews, for he found nothing faulty about Jesus. The enemy infiltrated the Jews to the extent that even at the request by Pilate to release Jesus Christ, they viciously objected to it (John 18:34-40).

---

[281] Ibid., 307-308.

[282] David Williams, "Judas Iscariot," in *Dictionary of Jesus and the Gospels* (Downers Grove: InterVarsity Press, 1992), 408.

During a heated argument between Pilate and the Jews on the release of Jesus Christ (John 19:1-5), the Jews cried out vehemently "Crucify him, crucify him. Pilate saith unto them, Take ye him, and crucify him: for I find no fault in him" (John 19:6). The battle of words went on until confused Pilate cautioned Jesus that he had power either to crucify him or to release him (John 19:10). Jesus spoke out to Pilate saying, "Thou couldest have no power at all against me, except it were given thee from above; therefore, he that delivered me unto thee have the greater sin" (John 19:11). Indeed, Pilate had no power over Jesus, but the Son of God was fully committed to obey the Father. Still Pilate was willing to release Jesus Christ, but the Jews craftily said, "If thou let this man go, thou art not Caesar's friend: whosoever maketh himself a king speaketh against Caesar" (John 19:12). The Jews wanted to antagonize Pilate to Caesar if he insisted on the release of Jesus. The Jews wanted Jesus to die and nothing else.

Finally, Jesus was "rejected as the Son of man, and the Son of God. Now we see him rejected as the Son of David (John 19:13-15)."[283] His own Jews wanted Him to die because they did not need Him. "The long trial was over. The die was cast. The stage was set for the final acts of this terrible drama."[284] "And he bearing his cross, went forth into a place called the place of a skull, which is called in the Hebrew Golgotha:"Where they crucified him, and two other with him, on either side one, and Jesus in the midst. And Pilate wrote a title, and put it on the cross. And the writing was, JESUS OF NAZARETH THE KING OF THE JEWS... in Hebrew, and Greek, and Latin (John 19:17-20).

Jesus was mocked by the soldiers, He was crucified on the cross, He died (Matt. 27:27-50), and was buried by "Joseph of Arimathaea, an honorable counselor, which also waited for the kingdom of God" (Mark 15:43). On the day Jesus Christ was crucified on Calvary "behold, the veil of the temple was rent in twain from the top to the bottom; and the earth did quake, and the rocks rent; And the graves were opened; and many bodies of the saints which slept arose...

---

[283] Phillips, 361.
[284] Ibid., 363.

Now when the centurion, and they that were with him, watching Jesus, saw the earthquake, and those things that were done, they feared greatly, saying, Truly, this was the Son of God" (Matt. 27:51-52). Those signs and the Spirit-led confession of the centurion, substantiate the deity of Jesus Christ as the Son of God.

Though Jesus predicted his death and resurrection on the third day (Mark 8:31; 9:31; 10:33), His disciples could not comprehend what He really meant, so some women went to the tomb to anoint His dead body (Mark 16:1). Entering into the sepulcher a divine agent said unto them, "Be not affrighted: Ye seek Jesus of Nazareth, which was crucified: he is risen; he is not here: behold the place where they laid him. But go your way, tell his disciples and Peter that he goeth before you in Galilee: there shall ye see him, as he said unto you" (Mark 16:6-7). As he predicted, He was raised on the third day (Mark 8:31; 9:31; 10:33). The death and resurrection of Jesus Christ is a dominant force, a humiliating move, and a victorious event over Satan and his kingdom. It is a demonstration of God's love through the One true Sacrifice of His Son on behalf of sin-polluted humanity.

Prior to His atoning death, Jesus cautioned, "And this gospel of the kingdom shall be preached in all the world for a witness unto all nations; and then shall the end come" (Matt. 24:14. The disciples should have taken Christ at His word, but they were not able to continue the Mission of Christ until the Holy Ghost would come upon them. The flesh would not survive the craftiness, wickedness, and violence of Satan. On the road To Emmaus Jesus appeared to His disciples.

Luke gives the following biblical account of the event:

> And said unto them, Thus it is written, and thus it behooved Christ to suffer, and to rise from the dead the third day: And that repentance and remission of sins should be preached in his name among all nations, beginning at Jerusalem. And ye are witnesses of these things, And, behold, I send the promise of my Father upon you; but tarry ye in the city of

Jerusalem, until ye be endued with power from on high." (Luke 24:46-49)

Jesus summarizes His earthly ministry. He had to stoop low to take up a human form, pay the penalty of death by dying on the cross, conquer death by resurrecting from the dead, so that His disciples would preach the gospel of the message of the kingdom of God to all nations with the condition that those who believe in Him would be forgiven their sins, cleansed, delivered from Satanic domain, and be born again. The Divine Agent to empower, lead, guide, and guard disciples of Jesus Christ for Spirit-anointed ministry is the Holy Ghost (John Chapters 15 and 16). Jesus, then implored His disciples to go and wait for the promise of the Father to pour out His Spirit upon them in Jerusalem; another Comforter and Counselor sent by the Father in the name of the Son Jesus Christ.

Giving the Great Commission to His disciples after His resurrection, Jesus said unto His disciples;

> Go ye into all the world, and preach the gospel to every creature. He that believeth and is baptized shall be saved; but he that believeth not shall be dammed. And these signs shall follow them that believe, in my name they shall cast out devils, they shall speak with new tongues; They shall take up serpents; and if they drink deadly thing, it shall not hurt them, they shall lay hands on the sick, and they shall recover. (Mark 16:15-18)

On the day of His ascension (after revealing Himself with convincing proof for forty days (Acts 1:1-6), Jesus said unto them, "It is not for you to know the times or the seasons, which the Father hath put in his own power, But ye shall receive power, after that the Holy Ghost is come upon you: and ye shall be witnesses unto me both in Jerusalem, and in all Judea, and in Samaria, and unto the uttermost part of the earth" (Acts 1:7-8). In contrast to Jesus' teaching about the kingdom of God, Peter's question about the kingdom of Israel opened yet another door for Jesus to teach the disciples about

His programmatic mission—the Mission of God. Emphasis is again placed on the endowment and empowerment of the Holy Ghost.

"And when he had spoken these things, while they were beheld, he was taken up; and a cloud received him out of their sight…two men stood by them in white apparel; Which also, said, Ye men of Galilee, why stand ye gazing up into heaven? this same Jesus, which is taken up from you into heaven, shall so come in like manner as ye have seen him go into heaven" (Acts 1:9-11). The Son went back to His Father (John 14:3, 12). His disciples should continue from where He ended, but they must be clothed and consumed by the Holy Ghost for effective witness of the Risen Jesus Christ by preaching the message of the kingdom of God to all nations amidst fierce and violent persecution. Watching the Master ascend into heaven, the angelic beings spoke about the descent of Jesus Christ as a confirmation to His earlier prediction (John 14:3). Jesus cautioned His disciples to continue the unfinished ministry of the risen Lord by preaching the kingdom of God in the power, leading, and prudence of the Holy Ghost.

The Holy Spirit

"In the OT the spirit *(ruah)* of Yahweh is God's power in action. Yahweh's spirit is God himself present at work, as are his 'hands' and his 'arms'."[285]

Parker shares some activities of Yahweh's Spirit:

> Yahweh's spirit is said to (1) shape creation, animate animals and mankind, and direct nature and history (Gen.1;2, 2:27; Pss. 104: 29-30). (2) reveal God's messages to his spokesmen (Neh. 9:30; Is. 61:1-4). (3) teach by these revelations the way to be faithful and fruitful (Pss. 143:10; Is. 63:10-14). (4) elicit faith, repentance, obedience, righteousness, docility, praise, and prayer (Pss. 51: 10-12; Joel 2:28-29; Zc. 12:10). (5) equip for strong, wise and effective

---

[285] Parker, "Holy Spirit," 316.

leadership (Gn. 41: 38; Dt. 34: 9; Jdg. 3:10; Is. 11:1-5). (6) give skill and application for creative work (Ex. 31:1-11; Hg. 2:5).[286]

The Spirit of Yahweh is actively involved in the Divine program—the affairs of the kingdom of God. The Spirit of God appropriates the day to day affairs to advance the kingdom of God.

Parker further unfolds the Personhood of the Spirit of God;

> In the NT, as in the LXX, spirit is pneuma, a word with similar association with ruah, and the Holy Spirit poured out by Christ at Pentecost (Jn. 1:33; Acts 2:33) is identified with the OT Spirit of God (Acts 2:16-21; 4:25; 7:51; 28:25; I Pet.1:11; 2 Pet. 1:19-21)...Over and above his previous functions, he is now given to the church as 'another (i.e. a second) Paraclete' (Jn. 14:16), taking over Jesus' role as counselor, helper, strengthener, supporter, adviser, advocate, ally (for the Gk. parakletos means all of these. Like the Father, and the Son, he acts as only a person can do—he hears, speaks, convinces, testifies, shows, leads, guides, teaches, prompts speech, commands, forbids, desires, helps, intercedes with groans (Jn. 14:26; 15:26; 16:7-15; Acts 2:4; 8:29; 13:2; 16:6-7; 21:11; Rom. 8:14, 16:26-27; Gal. 4:6; 5:17-18; Heb. 3:7; 10:15; I Pet. 1:11; Rev. 2:7, etc.).[287]

"John reports Jesus as saying that the Spirit's second-paraclete task is to mediate knowledge of, and union and communion with, the physically withdrawn, ascended and glorified Saviour (see Jn. 14:15-26; 16:14)."[288] Thus, the Holy Spirit draws sinful humanity into the family of God through genuine repentance and faith in

---

[286] Parker, 316.
[287] Ibid., 316-317.
[288] Ibid., 317.

Jesus Christ. He makes Christ real to believers in Christ. "As Jesus set out to convince and convict the world, which nevertheless did not "receive" him (1:12 etc.), so too the Paraclete's task is to convince and convict the world (Jn. 16:8-12),"[289] The word "another" used by Christ to qualify the Holy Spirit (the Paraclete, Advocate, Counselor) is clarified in this sense.

Jesus Christ cautioned His disciples to wait for the promise of the Father (Acts 1: 4). "John speaks of a coming gift of the Holy Spirit (14:26), or "Spirit of Truth" (14:17; 15:26; 16:13: cf. *Jud.* 25:14; *T. Jud.* 20:1-5; IQS 3:18-25), to act as a "paraclete" (*parakletos:* 14:16; 15:26; 16:7)."[290] German also adds that the "Paraclete is the Comforter (Counselor, Advocate)."[291] Jesus emphasized the coming of the Holy Spirit as very necessary and divine. Therefore, His disciples obeyed the command of their Master and tarried in the upper room eagerly anticipating the promised Holy Spirit. The disciples were not disappointed. The Holy Spirit did come upon the obedient disciples of the risen Savior and Lord Jesus Christ (Acts 2).

The First Century Believers in Jesus Christ

Pentecost is "a term derived from the Greek *pentekostos,* meaning fiftieth, which was applied to the fiftieth day after Passover. It was the culmination of the feast of weeks (Exod. 34:22; Deut. 16:10), which began on the third day after the presentation of the first harvest sheaves to God and which concluded with the offering of two loaves of unleavened bread representing the first products of the harvest (Lev. 23:17-20)."[292] Dr. Tenney further narrates that in the Christian church Pentecost is the anniversary of the coming of the Holy Spirit,[293] a fulfillment of Joel's prophecy (Joel 2:28-29).

---

[289] Max Turner, "Holy Spirit," in *Dictionary of Jesus and the Gospel* ed. Joel B. Green (Downers Grove: InterVarsity Press, 1992), 349.

[290] Turner, 350

[291] Terence German, "Holy Spirit," in *Evangelical Dictionary of Theology* ed. Walter A. Elwell (Grand Rapids: Baker Books, 1999), 523.

[292] Merrill Tenney, "Pentecost," in *Evangelical Dictionary of Theology* ed. Walter A. Elwell (Grand Rapids: Baker Books, 1999), 835.

[293] Ibid.

"As a group of 120 were praying in an upper room in Jerusalem fifty days after his death, the Holy Spirit descended upon them."[294] That day marked the birth of the New Testament church *(Acts 2:1-4)*—the church Jesus talked about based upon the revelatory truth through Peter that Christ is the Son of the living God (Matt. 16:13-18). The 120 were endowed with the power from on high (Luke 24:29; Acts 1:8)—not a human power, not a demonic power, not a mechanical power, but a Divine Agent with a supernatural power.

A multitudinous audience mocked the disciples as they spoke with other tongues. With great bewilderment amidst the mockery, the multitude who had come to partake of the Passover from various parts of the world could not believe their ears but subjected them to ridicule. They even thought the disciples had consumed too much new wine, thereby acting under the influence of alcohol (Acts 2:5-13).

Peter filled, baptized, and empowered by the Holy Spirit spoke with boldness and prudence of the Spirit—the "Revealer-Teacher"[295] Under the unique impulse of the Holy Spirit a former coward such as Peter boldly and courageously drew his audiences' attention to the word of God through the prophet Joel. Peter denied their naïve mind-set, indicating that they were not intoxicated, rather that was a manifestation of the descent of the Spirit of God upon them to carry on the mission of Christ—preaching the gospel of the kingdom of God to lost humanity, convicting them of their sins, converting them into the family of God, and preparing them for effective ministry (Eph. 4:11-15). In that powerful preaching of the kingdom of God, Peter confronted his audience with a heart-piercing conclusion (Acts 2:25-37).

Some of the bewildered audience were convicted at the powerful preaching of Peter (Acts 2:37). Those who were convicted of their spiritual nakedness and hunger, cried to the Spirit-anointed Disciples of Christ Jesus for what to do. Peter said that the Father's promise of the gift of the Holy Ghost is for all human beings who demonstrate sincere repentance of their sin and further express

---

[294] Ibid.,

[295] Turner, 350.

explicit faith in Jesus Christ. Not only the Jews, but both Jews and Gentiles (Acts 2:38-39).

In spite of Satan's deceptive move to subject Peter and the other disciples to ridicule, the Holy Spirit drew 3,000 souls into the family of God—the community of faith in Jesus Christ. These new believers in Christ enjoyed the gospel message, fellowship with one another in the ultimate fellowship of God, ate meals together, and prayed fervently (Acts 2:42).

The New Testament church grew spontaneously on the first day of the coming of "Another" Comforter, Revealer, Teacher, Paraclete, and Advocate—The Holy Spirit. "The concept of the kingdom of God implies a community."[296] Hence, those who responded positively to the preaching of the Kingdom constitute "the people of God, the Messianic community, the Body of Christ, the fellowship of the Spirit."[297] The biblical word 'church' (Gk. *ekklesia,* Heb, *qahal*) means "assembly."[298] The Holy Spirit inaugurated the church with unprecedented results. The Holy Spirit bonded the Messianic community together with an outstanding love and unity.

Though the concept of the kingdom of God is very broad "it must also be emphasized that kingship cannot be exercised in the abstract, but only over a people. The concept of the kingship of God implies both the existence of a group of people who own him as king and the establishment of a realm of people within which his gracious power is manifested."[299] The 120 believers in Christ who tarried in the upper room, including the 3,000 (excluding women and children) who also expressed their faith in Christ through confession and water baptism became subjects of the kingdom of God on the Day of Pentecost.

As Peter and John went to the temple, they came across a miserable lame man who begged for alms at the gate called Beautiful (Acts 3:1-2). As was his custom, the beggar beckoned to Peter and John for a token (Acts 3:3). Peter and John took that opportunity to

---

[296] I. Marshall, "Church," in *Dictionary of Jesus and the Gospels,* ed. Joel B. Green (Downers Grove: InterVarsity Press, 1992), 123.

[297] E., Clowney, 140-141.

[298] Ibid., 140.

[299] I. Marshall, 123.

speak the Name of the risen Lord and Savior into the deadly, deplorable, demeaning, and almost chronic circumstance of that messy lame man. "And Peter, fastening his eyes upon him with John, said, Look on to us. And he gave heed unto them, excepting to receive something of them" (Acts 3:4-5). Presumably, the lame beggar got ready to grab a coin (drakma) as usual. But there was a sharp shift of the normal gift of money—words the poor beggar had not heard before.

"Then Peter said, Silver and gold have I none; but in the name of Jesus Christ of Nazareth rise up and walk. And he took him by the right hand, and lifted him up: and immediately his feet and ankle bones received strength" (Acts 3:6-7). "The beggar, instead of his meager request, received a blessing that exceeded his fondest hope."[300] Thus, Peter "redirected the man's look away from himself to Jesus and offered him a new life in Christ.[301] The lame beggar was instantly healed (Acts 3:8-10). "With a joy that made him throw aside normal restraints, the beggar went leaping and shouting across the temple court."[302] The impotent received his strength and celebrated the victory of Jesus Christ in his former chaotic situation—a vivid demonstration of the ministry of the promised Holy Spirit through Peter and John—a bombshell, and an infringement upon the Satanic kingdom.

"Peter, who was never to miss an opportunity to proclaim his faith, saw his chance as the amazed crowd assembled."[303] Peter witnessed Jesus Christ under the unction, power, wisdom, and boldness of the Holy Spirit (Acts 3:11-26). Peter made it clear to his audience that though Pilate was convinced of no fault against Jesus Christ, but the Jewish Council and other Jews persuaded Pilate to convict Him of death by being hanged on the tree. Wade says the Jews rejected "the giver of life. They had chosen the taker of life, Barabbas, a murderer.[304] With embedded hatred the Jews rejected

---

[300] Wade, *Acts: Unlocking the Scriptures for You*, (37.

[301] Phillip, *Exploring Acts*, 68.

[302] Wade, 37.

[303] Ibid.,

[304] Ibid., 38.

the Lord and Savior their own prophets spoke about. They needed a "militant Messiah, one who would smash the power of Rome and make Jerusalem the capital of a new world empire. They were not interested in a meek Messiah."[305] The Holy Spirit moved Peter to expose their nakedness, naivety, stubborn refusal to obey the voice of Yahweh, false accusation of Jesus Christ that led to His crucifixion, and misconception of the coming Messiah—the Son of God, the Son of man, and the Son of David.

While some of the onlookers were bewildered by the radical change in the life of the former impotent, others were indignant about that outstanding healing miracle in the life of the lame beggar. This act of God's kindness through Peter and John infuriated Satan. As usual, the devil aggressively confronted Peter and John. The deceiver stirred the hearts and minds of the Jewish Council— the number one satanic human agents against Jesus Christ and his mission.

Did that act of God's kindness through Peter and John unto the lame man demand any brutal action against the two apostles (Peter and John)? Why were they summoned by the Sanhedrin? Phillips adds, "Peter's sermon contained an indictment of those who had killed Jesus...Clearly, Peter and John were too dangerous to be left loose to continue their preaching"[306] the gospel of the Kingdom of God. Satan persuaded his agents (the Jewish leaders) to pile up false charges against Peter and John in an effort to annihilate them as they did their Master a few months earlier, leading to His Crucifixion. Even in the midst of such persecution against the infant church, God gave increase—a declaration of His matchless power, sovereignty, and faithfulness even in perilous times (Acts 4:8-12).

To plot well against their demise the Jewish leaders locked Peter and John in jail until the following day when they appeared before the Jewish Council in Jerusalem (Acts 4:5-6). "And when they had set them in the midst, they asked, By what power, or by what name, have ye done this? (Acts 4:7) Undoubtedly, this was another great occasion to preach the message of the Kingdom to those spiritually

---

[305] Phillips, *Exploring Acts*, 75.

[306] Wade, *Acts: Unlocking the Scriptures for You*, (Cincinnati: OH Standard Publishing, 1991), 44-45.

poor people (Acts 4:8-12) who were influenced and pushed by Satan to carry on his nefarious deeds to revamp the cause of God.

The presence and power of the Holy Spirit was upon their lives. Human strength and wisdom could not have energized Peter and John to witness Jesus to the same Jewish leaders who killed the Christ. The "another" Paraclete, Advocate, Teacher, Counselor who was sent by the Father in the name of His Son Jesus Christ dominated and diminished their fears, nourished their faith in Christ, and used them to speak heart cutting words to persecutors of Jesus Christ and His church. "And by the hands of the apostles were many signs and wonders wrought among the people, and they were all with one accord in Solomon's porch...And believers were added to the Lord, multitudes both men and women" (Acts 5:12-14). Though the devil and his agents worked to revamp the cause of Christ, still more people came and accepted the preaching of the disciples, and became partakers of the Kingdom of God. Many miracles, signs, and wonders followed the disciples as they preached the Kingdom (Mark 16:15-20). Though the greatest miracle is salvation for sinners, the sick need healing, the lame need to walk, the blind need recovery of sight, demonic chains need to be broken, captives of Satan need deliverance, among many other supernatural move of the Holy Spirit. Hence, the urgent need for all believers in Christ to be empowered and equipped by the Holy Spirit for spiritual warfare cannot be underestimated or overlooked.

Satan intensified the spiritual warfare by inciting the high priest and the Sadducees against the Disciples of Christ (Acts 5:18). "The term "apostle" (*apostolos*) is used in the Gospels to designate the twelve disciples called and sent out by Jesus to preach the Gospel (*see* Gospel [Good News]) of the kingdom (*see* Kingdom of God) and demonstrate its presence by performing signs and wonders (*see* Miracles)."[307] Peter and John were among the twelve apostles accredited with miraculous signs and wonders. They were imprisoned because they taught in the name of Jesus with spontaneous and enormous results of a harvest of souls amidst diverse miracles.

---

[307] Colin Kruse, "Apostle," in *Dictionary of Jesus and the Gospels,* ed. Joel B. Green (Downers Grove: InterVarsity Press, 1992), 27.

The Jewish leaders grew bitter because the apostles taught in the name of Jesus, and even planned to slay the apostles, but Gamaliel, a doctor of law intervened on their behalf and said if the mission of the apostles was from God, then there was nothing the Jewish leaders could do to stop that God-led mission (Acts 5:22-39). Though Peter and John were subjected to flogging, that did not deter the disciples to preach and teach the message of the kingdom of God.

Wade puts it this way:

> The Sanhedrin's expectation that they could frighten the apostles into silence by beaten was in vain. The religious leaders expected the apostles to creep from the court in pain and disgrace. Instead, they left in triumph, rejoicing as they went. They were not masochists who derived a distorted sense of pleasure from physical suffering. They rejoiced because they were counted worthy of suffering for the name of Jesus. Nor did the beating they received keep them from preaching.[308]

Satan always raises death threats as violent instrument of spiritual warfare against the children of God, but unfortunately for him and his religious leaders in Jerusalem these apostles were not deterred by their ugly threats. Rather, they celebrated the Lord's victory over the arch enemy on their behalf and preached Jesus Christ with (Acts 5:41-42).

Jesus promised to build His church, and the gates of hell shall not prevail over it (Matt. 16:18) in spite of all odds against His cause. *"And Saul yet breathing out threatening and slaughter against the disciples of the Lord, went unto the high priest"* (Acts 9:1). Saul gave his approval about the stoning and subsequent death of Stephen (Acts 7:58). Saul's zeal was to bring all Disciples of Christ to Jerusalem to stand trial before the Jewish leaders and finally put to death (Acts 9:2). On the road to Damascus with letters

---

[308] Wade 62.

of authority from the high priest to bring disciples of Christ to stand before the Jewish Council in Jerusalem (Acts 9:2-3), the Lord of the church confronted him *(Acts 9:6-20)*. During that historic dialogue between Saul and Jesus Christ, the persecutor was called, chosen, commissioned, and given a command to advance in the kingdom of God (Acts 9:6-20).

> And straightway he preached Christ in the synagogues, that he is the Son of God. But all that heard him were amazed, and said, Is not this he that destroyed them which called on this name in Jerusalem, and came hither for that intent, that he might bring them bound unto the chief priests? But Saul increased the more in strength, and confounded the Jews which dwelt at Damascus, proving that this is very Christ."(Acts 9:20-22)

"With no conscious preparation, Paul found himself instantaneously compelled by what he saw and heard to acknowledge that Jesus of Nazareth, the crucified one, was alive after his passion, vindicated and exalted by God, and was now conscripting him into his service."[309] For some time the enemy used Saul to persecute the children of God, but now the One who owns the life of Saul delivered him from the wicked grips of Satan, and used him by the power and prudence of the Holy Spirit to witness Him—a strange turning point that could only be done by the Sovereign King of the Kingdom. Interestingly enough, Bruce says; "The Ethiopian could more easily change his skin or the leopard its spots that the arch-persecutor become a believer."[310] The spiritual warfare escalated as one of Satan's reliable and astute agent now preached and taught in the name of Jesus Christ.

"As they ministered to the Lord, and fasted, the Holy Ghost said, Separate me Barnabas and Saul for the work whereunto I have called them. And when they had fasted and prayed, and laid their hands on them, they sent them away. So they, being sent by the Holy Ghost,

---

[309] Bruce, *Paul: Apostle of the Heart Set Free*, (Grand Rapids: MI Eerdmans Publishing, 1997), 75.

[310] Ibid., 83.

departed unto Seleucia; and from thence they sailed to Cyprus (Acts 13:2-4), preaching the kingdom of God—the core message of the crucified, and the risen Jesus Christ. Saul planted many local assemblies, and he experienced fierce persecutions in diverse ways amidst miracles, signs, and wonders to confirm God's calling (e.g., Acts 16:16-40; 19:1-12; Acts 19:23-41; 23:12-26:32). Paul was a significant catalyst of growth in the first century church as well as in the contemporary church. Almost all the epistles in the New Testament were written by Paul. The Holy Spirit was the Divine agent behind Paul's vibrant ministry to advance the kingdom of God.

By the close of the first century A.D., Christianity (Acts 11:26; 26:28; I Pet. 4:16) "was well established in the Roman world. From its birthplace in Judaea it had spread west along the northern shore of the Mediterranean as far as Gaul, if not as far as Spain; it had spread along the North African coast to Cyrenaica."[311] McGrath also posits, "by the end of the first century, Christianity appears to have become established throughout the eastern Mediterranean world, and even to have gained a significant presence in the city of Rome, the capital of the Roman Empire."[312] The spread of Christianity to other nations was "partially through the efforts of early Christian evangelists such as Paul of Tarsus"[313] the apostle called to the Gentiles (Acts 9:15).

Though the arch-enemy of God and His Kingdom persistently oppose the advancement of the kingdom of God, Paul preached the kingdom of God and taught the things of Jesus Christ (Acts 28:26). "By tradition, Peter and Paul died during Nero's persecution of Christians after the great fire in Rome in 64 C. E."[314] Christianity overwhelmingly thrived through martyrdom, and various degrees of persecution to bring in the sheaves from the wallowing mire and dominion of Satan. Though the was alarming resistance to further the Kingdom of God the first century believers in Jesus Christ were anointed, empowered and led by the Holy Spirit to draw men and women into the family of God.

---

[311] Bruce, *New Testament History*, 415.

[312] McGrath, 5.

[313] Ibid.

[314] Matthews, 291.

CHAPTER 6

DIVERSE DOCTRINES AND PRAXIS OF THE KINGDOM OF GOD IS SPIRITUAL WARFARE

Weak and Weird Ecclesiological Doctrines and Praxis

I liken the kingdom of God to the sea. Very broad with myriads of sea creatures in it, some are edible, while others are not. Still, some are very tiny, while others are huge. The Church is very broad with myriads of sects, denominations, among others. Looking through the spiritual magnifying glass of the Christian Holy Bible some are children of God by faith in Jesus Christ (John 1:18; 3:16; 3:36; 10:9-10) and for that matter subjects of the kingdom of God while a vast majority do not subscribe to the exclusive Lordship Jesus Christ as the Son of God—the Savior. Therefore, under the sub-heading "weak and weird ecclesiological doctrines and praxis" attention is focused on the difference between the doctrines and praxis of the faithful remnant of the kingdom of Christ and God (Eph. 5:5), and the majority who deny the deity of the King of the Kingdom—Jesus Christ.

"While Christianity recognizes that the promise of a personal, spiritual savior is the core of biblical revelation, Judaism has long vacillated in its concept of messiahship."[315] Interestingly enough, "from the time of Jesus of Nazareth until Moses Hayyim Luzatto (died A. D. 1747), there have been at least thirty-four different prom-

---

[315] Josh McDowell and Don Stewart, *Handbook of Today's Religions* (Nashville, TN: Thomas Nelson Publishers, 1983), 372.

inent Jews who have claimed to be the Messiah"[316]—a substantial evidence that Judaism does not recognize Jesus Christ of Nazareth as the Messiah of whom the prophets spoke. Ignorantly, Judaism is still waiting for a Messiah. In Judaism "atonement is accomplished by sacrifices, penitence, good deeds and a little of God's grace. No concept of substitutionary atonement (as in Christianity in the Person of Jesus Christ) exists."[317] In the tradition of "Hasidism, or "pious ones"[318]—a faction in Judaism," a Zaddik, or holy man, can become a channel for God's saving power. He is a power in himself and can inspire enlightenment in others."[319] The aforementioned sampling of doctrines and praxis of Judaism is hollow, weak, and weird—a vivid illustration that the Kingdom of God is spiritual warfare.

The doctrines and praxis of the kingdom of God by Roman Catholicism is equally weak and weird in the light of God and the Christian Holy Bible. "At the Council of Ephesus (431) Mary was declared to be the Mother of God *(Theotokos)* and not only the mother of Christ *(Christokotos)*. This gave an impetus to Marian devotion and by the seventh century four Marian feasts were being observed in Rome: the annunciation, the purification, the assumption, and the nativity of Mary."[320] Piggins advocates that "the dogmas of papal primacy and infallibility were promulgated as recently as Vatican I (1869-70)."[321] Still another heretical doctrine and praxis of Roman Catholicism is "a supposed middle state between heaven and hell (*cf.* Eschatology*)."[322] The above

are but a few extracts from various heresies that back the concept of the Kingdom of God is spiritual warfare.

As a cult, "the Mormon Church teaches that Christianity was in apostasy for some 18 centuries until God revealed new "truth" to

---

[316] Ibid.

[317] McDowell and Stewart, 373.

[318] Matthews, 261.

[319] Ibid.

[320] F. S. Piggin, "Roman Catholicism," in *Evangelical Dictionary of Theology*, ed. Walter A. Elwell (Grand Rapids: Baker Books, 1999), 958.

[321] Ibid., 956.

[322] R. T. Beckwith, "Purgatory," in *New Dictionary of Theology*, ed. Sinclair B. Ferguson (Downers Grove: InterVarsity Press, 1988), 549.

Joseph Smith, Jr.[323] "Also known as the Church of Jesus Christ of Latter Day Saints, the Mormon Church has their so-called sacred literature called The Book of Mormons."[324] They ascribe to those books as their final word of authority instead of the Christian Holy Bible. McDowell and Stewart conclude, "the "Jesus" of the cults is always someone less than the Bible's eternal God who became flesh, lived here on earth, and died for our sins,"[325] and rose back from the dead for our justification (Rom. 4:25). In view of the foregoing, the doctrines and the praxis of the Mormon Church are weak and weird—unbiblical and unfounded.

Another cult in this discussion is the Jehovah's Witness. McDowell and Stewart assert that Jehovah's Witnesses believe and teach that "the biblical doctrine of the Holy Trinity, one God in three Persons, is pagan or Satanic in origin."[326] Denial of the Holy Trinity is denial of the One True God—the Father, the Son, and the Holy Spirit.

The founder of the Unification Church "Moonies" Sun Myung Moon "claims that Jesus Christ appeared to him in the vision admonishing him to carry on the task Christ had failed to complete."[327] Moon claims "himself to be Messiah for this age."[328] Interestingly, Moon who frowns at the redemptive work of Christ admits that it was Christ who revealed Himself to him (Moon)—a conflicting assertion that sabotages Moon's weird claims, doctrine, and praxis of the kingdom of God.

Doctrines and Praxis of World Religions

The doctrines and praxis of all world religions adequately demonstrate that the Kingdom of God is spiritual warfare. Islam, Buddhism, Satanism, and Hinduism are briefly highlighted for the sake of space.

---

[323] McDowell and Stewart, 20.

[324] Ibid., 21.

[325] Ibid., 22.

[326] Ibid., 23.

[327] Ibid., 99.

[328] Ibid.

"The five articles of faith are the main doctrines of Islam: There is only one true God and his name is Allah. Allah is all-knowing, all-powerful and the sovereign judge. Yet Allah is not a personal God, for he is so far above man in very way that he is not personally knowable"[329] unlike the God of Christians who dwells in the heaven but resides in the hearts of His children. According to Islam the Qur'an (their sacred literature) supersedes all books including the Bible. "Muhammad is the last and the greatest of all the six prophets (Adam, Noah, Abraham, Moses, and Jesus)."[330] Islam teaches that on the last day "those who follow and obey Allah and Muhammad will go to Islamic heaven, called Paradise, a place of pleasure, while the disobedient will go to hell in torments."[331] The aforementioned and many more false beliefs and teachings of Islam are used by the devil to wage war against God and His Kingdom.

"The Buddhist world view is basically monistic—that is, the existence of a personal creator and Lord is denied. The world operates by natural power and law, not a divine command. There are those who deify the Buddha but along with him they worship other gods."[332] Buddhists have their own sacred literature known as "The Three Baskets." [333] The literature, doctrines and praxis of Buddhists are mythically weird, and have no place in the kingdom of God.

Another deceptive religion is Satanism. McDowell says; "Black magic, the Black Mass, facets of drug culture, and blood sacrifice all have connections with Satanism."[334] "Although the church of Satan sounds like a contradiction in terms, it was founded in San Francisco in 1966 by Anton Szandor La Vey"[335] the church gives prominence to materialism and self-satisfaction. It is very regrettable that the church of Satan believes and teaches that "Satan is more of a symbol

---

[329] McDowell and Stewart, 389.

[330] Ibid., 390.

[331] Ibid.

[332] McDowell and Stewart, 320.

[333] Ibid., 310.

[334] Ibid., 237.

[335] Ibid.,

than a reality."³³⁶ The devil has convinced and deceived Satanism that he is not real. This misconception grips them to defend their master (Satan) in all his deeds against humanity. Satanism espouses any type of sexual activity that satisfies one's need—heterosexuality, homosexuality, adultery or unfaithfulness in marriage.

Lastly in my list is Hinduism. "The Hindu scriptures, written over a period of 2,000 years (1400 B.C.-500 AD) are voluminous.³³⁷ Their scriptures contain myriads of weird doctrines and praxis, such as, "one's present state of existence is determined by his [or her] performance in previous lifetimes. "The law of karma is the law of moral consequences or the effect of any action upon the performer in a past... As one performs righteous acts, he [or she] moves towards liberation from the cycle of successive births and deaths. Contrariwise, if one's deeds are evil, he [or she] will move further from liberation."³³⁸ The doctrines and praxis of Hinduism are opposed to biblical concept of the Kingdom of God is spiritual warfare.

Christocentric Doctrines and Praxis

Extensive discussion is contained in previous chapters hence brief highlights are tabulated under the current subheading:

1. The Christian Holy Bible is inspired by God (II Tim 3:16; I Pet. 1:20).
2. God is the Creator of the heaven and the earth (Gen. 1:1) (a) birds of the air, and fish and other sea creatures (Gen 1:20-23), (b) cattle and all creeping creatures (Gen. 1:24-25).
3. God created humanity in His image and likeness (Adam and Eve) (Gen. 1:26-31).
4. Marriage is between a man and a woman (Gen. 1:27; 2:21-24; Matt. 19:1-6).
5. Adam and Eve fell as a result of their disobedience to God in the Garden of Eden (Gen. 3).

---

³³⁶ Ibid., 238.

³³⁷ Ibid., 284.

³³⁸ Ibid. 289.

6. There is only One True God who reveals Himself in three Persons the Father, the Son, and the Holy Ghost (Matt. 28:19).
7. The Deity of Jesus Christ—His virgin birth (Isa. 7: 14; 9: 6-7; Luke 1: 26-38), His sinless life (II Cor. 5:21), His miracles (Mark 1:21-45), His atoning death and burial (Matt. 27:32-60), His bodily resurrection (Matt. 28:1-20), His ascension to the Father in heaven (Acts 1:9-11a), and His second Coming to take His Church (John 14:1-3; Acts 1:11b).
8. The Person and ministry of the Holy Spirit (John 16:7-15; Acts 1:8).
9. The Holy Spirit Baptism (Matt. 3:11; Acts 2: 1-4; 10: 45-47; 19:6).
10. The Great Commission—Biblical assignment of the Church to preach and teach the message of the kingdom of God to all nations (Matt. 28:19; Mark 16:15-18; Luke 24:46-48; John 20:21; Acts 1:8).
11. Salvation is through faith in Jesus Christ (John 3:16; Acts 4:12; Rom. 10:9-10).
12. The Ordinances of the Church; (a) Water baptism for those who repent of their sins and accept the gift of salvation through faith in Jesus Christ (Matt. 28:19; Acts 8:34-38). (b) The Lord's Supper/Communion/The Lord's Table (Matt. 26:26-28; I Cor. 11:23-26).
13. God expects a perpetual life of holiness from all who receive Jesus Christ as Lord and Savior (John 17:17).
14. Believers in Jesus Christ are born by the Spirit of God (John 1:18).
15. Miracles, signs, and wonders follow believers in Jesus Christ (Mark 16:16-20; Acts).
16. Believers in Christ are the salt of the earth...the light of the world (Matt. 15:13-16).
17. "The Kingdom of God creates the church"[339] the Body of Christ (Col. 1:24).
18. Believers in Jesus Christ cheerfully give a tenth of their income (tithe) to the cause of God (Mal. 3:10), as well as offering (II Cor. 9:6-7).

---

[339] Ladd, 611.

19. Children of the Kingdom of God worship the Lord is spirit and in truth (John 4:24) with musical instruments (Ps. 150), pray and fast (Matt. 17:21), and pray without ceasing (Luke 18:1-8; I Thess. 5:17) in the Name of Jesus Christ (John 14:12-14).
20. Satan, also known as the serpent, the devil, the intruder, the deceiver, the liar, the slanderer, and the tempter is a real creature (not a myth). God will finally destroy him and his demonic agents, and all unbelievers in His (God's) appointed time (Rev. 20:10-15).
21. The Blessed Hope when Jesus Christ comes to rapture His Church (I Thess. 16-17).
22. The Millennial reign of Jesus Christ (Rev. 20: 1-6).
23. The New Heavens and the New Earth (Rev. 21).
24. Believers in Jesus Christ are more than conquerors in Him (John 19:30; Acts 2:23-24; Col. 2:15; Cor. 15:57; Rom 8:37-39).

CHAPTER 7

THE CONSUMATION OF THE KINGDOM OF GOD IS SPIRITUAL WARFARE

Pre-Second Advent of Jesus Christ

*J*esus promised to come back for His Church (John 14:1-3). He also cautions His disciples to be vigilant during the time of waiting for His coming. Again, Jesus unfolds a revelation on the issue of His coming after He had lamented on the plight of Jerusalem (Matt. 24:1-14). Jesus gave a clue with diverse happenings or events prior to His second advent. All the signs Jesus gave are on being unfolded daily—testifying the authenticity of the sayings of the Son of God. Three paramount issues are discussed under this subject.

First, the love of some disciples of Jesus Christ will wax cold because of the enormity of evil deeds. The message of the Lord of the Church to the seven churches in Asia (Rev. Chapters 2-3) is applicable to every generation of the community of faith in Jesus Christ. Jesus addresses various fleshy deeds such as self-abasement, self-complacency, self-righteousness, self-sufficiency, among other self egos, but He warns the saints to desist from self lusts and cleave to genuine and wholesome worship of God. The Lord of the Church suffered persecution right from His earthly birth (Matt. 2:13-23) to Crucifixion. His Church also suffered persecution at its birth (Acts 2:13; Chapters 3-4). The Church still suffers persecution in diverse ways, but Christ warns that through persistent faith in Him victory is assured.

Second, "...this gospel of the kingdom shall be preached in all the world for a witness unto all nations; and then shall the end come." (Matt. 24:14). Jesus wants all peoples to hear the message of the Kingdom of God and respond affirmatively to the gift of salvation through faith in Him. Bosch argues that "Jesus inaugurated the Kingdom, but He did not bring it to consummation."[340] The message of the Kingdom is confrontational against the devil and his agents; it uncovers the deep secret thoughts of both the mind and the heart of humanity. It is the Sword of the Spirit to counterattack the fiery darts and lies of Satan. I agree with Paul, "...I am not ashamed of the gospel of Christ: for it is the power of God unto salvation to everyone that believeth, to the Jews first, and also to the Greek" (Rom. 1:16). Jesus wants His Church to preach the gospel to open the eyes of the blind and lead them from darkness, doom, and destruction to the marvelous kingdom of light and life.

Third, Jesus wants believers in him (subjects of the kingdom of God) to prepare for His silent coming to fulfill His promise (John 14:6). The "rapture of the Church,' a phrase used by premillenialists to refer to the church being united with Christ at His second coming (from the Lat. rapino, "caught up")...(I Thess. 4:15-17),"[341] thus, "The Blessed Hope—When Jesus raptures His Church prior to His return to earth—-the second coming. "At this future moment in time all believers who have died will rise from their graves and will meet the Lord in the air, and Christians who are alive will be caught up with them, to be with the Lord forever."[342] Prior to this glorious event the enemy intensifies his persecution just to diminish the faith of believers in the Lord. Therefore, Jesus warns believers in

---

[340] David Bosch, *Transforming Mission: Paradigm Shift in Theology of Mission* (Mary Knoll, NY: Orbis Books, 2009), 35.

[341] R. G. Clouse, "Rapture of the Church," in *Evangelical Dictionary of Theology*, ed. by Walter A. Elwell (Grand Rapids: Baker Books, 1999), 908.

[342] Assemblies of God Michigan District "Our Beliefs" http://www.aogmi.org/beliefs (Accessed on November 25, 2013).

Him to persist in their faith by being sensitive to the voice, promptings, and leading of the indwelt Holy Spirit—"the Comforter" (John 15:26; 16:7).

Post-Second Advent of Jesus Christ

After healing the man at the pool of Bethesda the Jews became very indignant because they accused Jesus of breaking the Sabbath and also making himself equal with God (John 5:1-18). John records Jesus' interpretation of the consummation of the kingdom of God:

> Verily, verily, I say unto you, He that heareth my word, and believeth on him that sent me, hath everlasting life, and shall not come into condemnation; but is passed from death unto life. Verily, verily, I say unto you, The hour is coming, and now is come when the dead shall hear the voice of the Son of God; and they that hear shall live. For as the Father has life in himself, And hath given him authority to execute judgment also, because he is the Son of man. Marvel not at this; for the hour is coming, in the which all that are in the grave shall hear his voice. And shall come forth; they that have done good, unto the resurrection of life; and they that have done evil, unto the resurrection of damnation. (John 5:24-29)

This prophetic word of Jesus Christ refers to the actual consummation of the kingdom of God. This event is "the millennial reign of Christ when Jesus returns with His saints at His second coming and begins His benevolent rule over 1,000 years.[343] Satan would not have any power again to persecute believers in Christ through diverse torments and torture—he would be bound for that period of 1,000 years (Rev. 20:2-6).

---

[343] Ibid.,

Those who reject Christ prior to His second visible return and reign with the saints for a thousand years would be judged. John writes:

> "And the devil that deceived them was cast into the lake of fire and brimstone, where the beast and false prophets are, and shall be tormented day and night-forever and ever. And I saw a great white throne, and him that sat on it, from whose face the earth and the heaven fled away; and there was found no place for them. And I saw the dead, small and great, stand before God; and the books were opened; and another book was opened, which is the book of life: and the dead were judged, out of those things which were written in the books, according to their works. And the sea gave up the dead which were in it; and death, and hell delivered up the dead which were in them: and they were judged every man according to their works. And death and hell were cast into the lake of fire. This is the second death. And whosoever was not found written in the book of life was cast into the lake of fire." (Rev. 20:10-15)

The lake of fire "is the place of eternal punishment for the wicked. The beast and false prophets are thrown alive into it before the millennial reign (Rev. 19:20). After the final battle they are joined by Satan (Rev. 20:10), and after the final judgment Death and Hades are also cast in (Rev.20:14; cf. Isa. 25:8; I Cor. 115:26) as well as those whose names are not in the book of life (Rev. 20:15) and evil men (Rev. 21:8)."[344]

Mounce says;

> Rev. 20:14 and 21:8 equate the lake of fire with the second death (cf. Rev. 2:11; 20:6), a rabbinic term for the death of the wicked in the next world. After

---

[344] W. Mounce, "Lake of Fire," in *Evangelical Dictionary of Theology*, ed. Walter A Elwell (Grand Rapids: Baker Books, 1999). 617-618.

> physical death (i.e., the first death) the soul resides temporarily in Hades and goes through the final judgment. The wicked are then condemned to the lake of fire (i.e., the second death) in eternal conscious punishment (cf. Rev. 20:10; 14:11). There is no concept of annihilation in Revelation.[345]

Naturally, fire can easily annihilate a human being into ashes, but this particular lake of fire torments and tortures the wicked but does not eradicate those who are put in it. Thus, the consummation of the Kingdom of God gets to its climax with Satan and all his spiritual and physical agents thrown into the unquenchable lake of fire forever.

The new Heaven and the new Earth follows the millennial reign of Christ and the saints on earth. "And I saw a new heaven and a new earth: for the first heaven and the first earth were passed away; and there was no more sea" (Rev. 21:1)—a mystery that is actualized by the Creator of the universe; the One who created the world out of nothing is more than able to remove the old order and replace it with a new order. "Satan and his followers [both spiritual and physical] have traded the new creation for the lake of fire."[346] Satan and his allies voluntarily chose to disobey, rebel, and fight against the will of the Sovereign God—their destiny is everlasting doom and destruction; perpetual anguish and agony (Rev. 21:1-8).

The tormentor is now in torments. The torturer is now being tortured. The arrogant is now humbled and humiliated. The saints of God are free from demonic attacks persecution, and oppression. The King advocates the authenticity of His words. He comforts, and consoles His subjects. While the saints—the obedient and faithful ones are assured of personal communion with God in new Heaven and the new Earth the wicked suffers eternal damnation in the lake of fire.

---

[345] Ibid., 618.

[346] Mounce, 618.

CONCLUSION

Who among creation can battle with the Creator God and triumph? Absolutely, no spirit, flesh, dominion, power, name nor title can triumph over the self-existing God. Lucifer, also known as Satan, lured humanity (people God created in His image and likeness), and castigated God to be a liar in the face of Eve (Gen. 3:4-5). The deceiver spearheaded the voluntary disobedience of Adam and Eve, and craftily diverted their attention from God to himself—spiritual warfare. "The conflict between Satan and man [humanity] which began in the garden will most assuredly end with God's total victory"[347] for the Lord is strong and mighty in all battles (Ps. 24:8-10). "We already know who wins. If we forget that, we may start reacting to Satan as if he were the ultimate winner instead of the ultimate loser. Satan was defeated the instant he rebelled against God."[348] Ignorance of Christ's victory over Satan and his allies is a defeat in itself, and believers in Christ must not be ignorant of this biblical and theological truth.

Outrageous persecutions of believers in Christ by the devil in various forms must not be misconstrued as victory for Satan. Though there is ongoing warfare between Satan and humanity, those who persevere in their faith in Christ Jesus will enjoy eternity with God. "God makes it possible for us [all believes in His Son Jesus Christ] to encounter and overcome our suffering…He makes it possible for us [the faithful remnant] to have a complete and purposeful

---

[347] Mounce, 618

[348] Evans, 208.

Christian life."[349] Jesus' assurance to His disciples is still in force. "I am with you always, even unto the end of the world" (Matt. 28:20b). The enemy can't go beyond where God allows him to go neither can he outdo what the Lord does not permit him to do. Suffering for the sake of Christ and gospel of the Kingdom is rewarding now and future. God wipes away tears of sorrow of those who faithfully and persistently partake in advancing the Kingdom.

I am challenging you to understand the detail of spiritual warfare, so that you can comprehend the conflict in which you are in. I am not infusing cowardice in you to fear the devil. Rather, I am convinced and led by the Holy Spirit to create your awareness of the ongoing warfare waged by Satan in and against you. Many Christians are very ignorant about Satan (the architect and authority behind spiritual warfare). Identifying who the devil is, his deadly schemes and deeds, and your preparation to counteract his offensive weaponry with biblical and theological approach appropriates a victories life in Jesus Christ. "We are at war. The Captain of our salvation has delegated to us authority over 'all the powers of the evil one' (Luke 10:17-19). Yet Satan and his demons, though defeated by the Lord on our behalf, are not dead;"[350] they aggressively seek to devour humanity especially the community of faith in Christ (I Pet. 5:8). You are summoned to extreme vigilance of the ongoing spiritual warfare "Lest Satan should get an advantage of us; for we are not ignorant of his devices" (2 Cor. 2:11). There is no room for you to either underestimate or overestimate Satan and his fierce battle against God and His Kingdom.

Jesus has given His Church a Commission popularly called the Great Commission (Matt. 28:18; Mark 16:15-18; Luke 24:47-49; John 20:21; Acts 1:8). "What Jesus began 'both to do and say' is now the ministry he has left his church until he comes again. The mission is that of Jesus himself—God's kingdom has having come as good news for the poor. But the empowering for the kingdom, as then, is the continuing work of the [Holy] Spirit."[351] The sacred

---

[349] Jim Anderson, *Philosophy: As Viewed Through A Biblical Lens* (Omaha, NB: Anderson Evangelistic Enterprises, 1994), 164.

[350] Murphy, 537.

[351] Murray Dempster, Byron Klaus, and Douglas Petersen, *Called & Empowered: Global Mission in Pentecostal Perspective* (Peabody, MA: Hendricks Publishers, 2008), 18.

obligation given to the church by Jesus Christ would not be effectively appropriated without recognition of the Person, ministry, and active involvement of the Holy Spirit. Jesus "was anointed by the Holy Spirit precisely for such a mission; and he in turn poured out the Spirit on his disciples so that they [we] might continue that same mission."[352] The church's accomplishment will be very insignificant in the eyes of God if it (the church) does not embrace the infilling, empowerment, anointing, and leading of the Holy Spirit.

The church is mandated "to proclaim the legacy of its Master, but in dynamic forms. Every age has to find its own appropriate forms for expressing the ever-relevant message of Jesus on the kingdom of God. The forms may change but the essence remains."[353] The Holy Spirit equips believers in Christ to reach out with the message of the Kingdom, bind demonic allies, pull down strongholds of the enemy, and loose captives of Satan (II Cor. 10:3-6) to enable all peoples hear the good news of the Kingdom (Matt. 24:14), confess and forsake their sins, accept the gift of salvation through faith in Jesus Christ, and experience perpetual victory in their quest to advance the Kingdom of God.

One of the manifestations of a persistent victorious life in Christ Jesus is praise and gratitude to God. "Bless the LORD, O my soul: and all that is within me, bless his holy name. Bless the LORD, O my soul, and forget not all his benefits"(Ps. 103:1-2). "Praise ye the LORD, Praise, O ye servants of the LORD, praise the name of the LORD" (Ps. 113:1). "Praise may be defined as homage rendered to God by his creatures [believers in Christ] in worship of his person and in thanksgiving for his favors and blessings."[354] Jesus in four occasions publicly expressed gratitude to the Father in heaven (John 11:38-44; 14:16-19; Luke 10:17-24 Matt. 26:26-27). "Whoso offereth praise glorify me: and to him that ordereth his conversation aright will I will I show the salvation of God" (Ps. 50:23). Praise

---

[352] Ibid.

[353] Caragounis, 430.

[354] G. Stanton, "Prayer," in *Evangelical Dictionary of Theology*, ed. Walter A. Elwell (Grand Rapids: Baker Books, 1999), 865.

accompanies preaching and teaching the Kingdom to touching and transforming lives in the power of the Holy Spirit. Perpetual life of praise triggers supernatural works of the sovereign King. Praise is healing to body, soul, and spirit. The arch enemy cannot stand the power of praise and worship to God. Put the devil to flight with a constant atmosphere of praise and worship not only in time of abundance and breakthrough, but also in time of lack and seemingly impenetrable challenges. Praise and worship prevails over all satanic resistance, and explodes outstanding miracles (Acts 16:16-40).

"Watch and pray, that ye enter not into temptation: the spirit indeed is willing, but the flesh is weak" (Matt. 26:41). Prayerlessness is demon-dominance, self-centeredness, self-sufficiency, self-conceited, and self- dependent. "We are called to present personal and individual needs to God, but at the same time we are urged to intercede for the whole company of the saints (John 17:20-21; Eph. 6:18) and also for the world at large (I Tim. 2:1-2)."[355] Holy Spirit-led prayer in the Name of Jesus Christ is a dominant force that counterattacks the works of the enemy, subdues his authority, crashes down strongholds, and delivers captives from unbelief, fear, addictions, pride, and other fiery darts of the devil. Effective prayer melts the spiritual demonic shackles around the hearts of unbelievers and points their focus and allegiance to the exclusive Lordship of Jesus Christ. Preaching, teaching, witnessing, counseling, and other ministry programs to advance the Kingdom of God is deficient without the inevitable ingredient of Spirit-anointed prayer in the Name of Jesus Christ.

I vehemently advocate and fervently practice biblical and theological fasting (e.g., II Chron. 20:1-30; Joel 2; Matt. 4:2; Acts 13:2-3). I am opposed to starvation, hunger strike, and other demonic abstinence from food (e.g. Acts 23: 12-14). In the church of our day "food for the body" is highly embraced more than "faith in Jesus Christ." In my own estimation the word "fasting" is frowned at by 85% of partakers of the Kingdom of God. Majority of believers in Christ have inclined and aligned their loyalty to the enemy by wholeheartedly deducing that "fasting" is not biblical and theological.

---

[355] D. Bloesch, "Praise," 867.

CONCLUSION

Fasting even rooted or neglected out of many if not all Bible translations or versions with the exception of King James that quotes the direct answer of Jesus Christ to His disciples of their inability to cast out a demon from a lunatic (Matt. 17:14-20); "Howbeit this kind goeth not out but by prayer and fasting." (Matt. 17:21 KJV). Dr. Williams adds that "Fasting is a miracle cleanser…it does not change God; it changes us and prepares us for spiritual revelation. It brings us into a spiritual position that amplifies and concentrates the power of God working in us."[356] But the devil constantly disengage many believers in Christ Jesus to underrate "fasting" thereby depriving them from maintaining spiritual and physical vitality and sensitivity to the voice and direction of the Holy Spirit.

If you have not accepted the gift of salvation through faith in Jesus Christ, I am urgently counseling you not to be deceived again with hollow and naïve theories, philosophies, and myths; "For God loved the world, that he gave his only begotten Son, that whosoever believeth in him should not perish, but have everlasting life"(John 3:16). The Only One who accomplished your (humanity) victory over Satan, sin, and death extends a matchless and rewarding invitation to you. He says; "Come unto me, all that labor and are heavy laden, and I will give you rest. Take my yoke upon you, and learn from me; for I am meek and lowly in heart: and ye shall find rest unto your souls. For my yoke is easy, and my burden is light" (Matt. 10:28-30). A former zealous persecutor of Christ and His Church Paul says, "But for us also, to whom it shall be imputed, if we believe on him that raised up Jesus our Lord from the dead. Who was delivered for our offences, and was raised again for our justification" (Rom. 4:24-25).

A former stanch idol worshipper who frowned and mocked at the teachings of the Kingdom of God, an extreme alcoholic, and a chain smoker like me (the author of the book in your hand), I challenge you to embrace the matchless love of God for you, His long suffering for you, the victory He won on your behalf, and His incomparable power that is available for you to triumph through traumatic times in your life. The compassionate and loving God

---

[356] Dave Williams, *The Miracle Results of Fasting: Your Secret Weapon in Spiritual Warfare* (Lansing MI: Decapolis Publishing, 1997), 52-54.

welcomes all peoples irrespective of color, gender, nationality, ethnicity, race, societal status, religious background, into His Kingdom through faith in His Son Jesus Christ. To be part of this vibrant winning contingent of God, sincerely repent and confess your sins to God by faith through Jesus Christ (John 14:6; John 10:9) for forgiveness, cleansing, deliverance, and be imputed with the righteousness that comes from God (II Cor. 5:21). Prayerfully consider becoming a committed member of a Bible believing and Christ centered church, nurture your newfound faith in Christ with the Word of God in humility and obedience, appropriate the triumph of the King in your daily battle with satanic forces, and fulfill God's calling on your life as a Spirit-led warrior in the Kingdom of God.

BIBLIOGRAPHY

Alexander, Paul. "The Battle of Ideas, Concepts, and Thoughts." *Spiritual Warfare in Enrichment: Enriching and Equipping Spirit-filled Ministers 18, no. 3* (June 2013): 66-70.

Allen, Leslie. "*Rom. 8:14-17.*" *Zondervan Bible Commentary,* edited by F. F. Bruce. Grand Rapids: Zondervan, 2008.

Anderson, Jim. *Philosophy: As Viewed Through A Biblical Lens,* Omaha, NB: Anderson Evangelistic Enterprise, 1994.

Assemblies of God Michigan District. "Our Beliefs." www.aogmi.org/beliefs (Accessed November 25, 2013).

Baker, David. "God, Names of." In *Dictionary of Old Testament Pentateuch,* edited by T. Desmond Alexander, 359-368. Downers Grove: InterVarsity Press, 2003.

Barker, Kenneth and John Kohlenberger III. *Zondervan NIV Bible Commentary Vol. 2. New Testament.* Grand Rapids: Zondervan, 1994.

Barclay, O. "World." In *New Dictionary of Theology,* edited by Sinclair Ferguson, 729-730. Downers Grove: InterVarsity Press, 1988.

Bauer, D. "Son of God." In *Dictionary of Jesus and the Gospels,* edited by Joel B Green, 769-775. Downers Grove: InterVarsity Press, 1992.

_____ "Son of David." In *Dictionary of Jesus and the Gospels,* edited by Joel B. Green, 766-769. Downers Grove: InterVarsity Press, 1992.

Beckwith, R. "Purgatory." In *New Dictionary of Theology,* edited by Sinclair Ferguson, 549-550. Downers Grove: InterVarsity Press, 1988.

Bloesch, Donald. "Prayer." In *Evangelical Dictionary of Theology,* edited by Walter A. Elwell, 866-868. Grand Rapids: Baker Books, 1999.

_____"Praise." In *Evangelical Dictionary of Theology,* edited by Walter A. Elwell, 865-866. Grand Rapids: Baker Books, 1999.

Boateng, Richard A. "Prospects of the Economic Community of West African States Standby Force"(MAMAS, thesis., US Army Command and General Staff College, 2006).

Boredom Blamed for Murders: A True Killing Impulse? http://www.nbcnews.com/health/boredom-blamed-murders-true-killing-impulse-6C10963043 (Accessed August 22, 2013).

Bosch, David. *Transforming Mission: Paradigm Shift in Theology of Mission.* Maryknoll, NY: Orbis Books, 2009.

Branch, Robin. "Sarah." In *Dictionary of Old Testament Pentateuch,* edited by T. Desmond Alexander, 733-736. Downers Grove: InterVarsity Press, 2003.

Brantford, James. "Keep on Praying for All the Saints: Intercession and Spiritual Warfare." *Spiritual Warfare in Enrichment: Enriching and Equipping Spirit-filled Ministers 18 No. 3* (June 2013): 54-58.

Bromiley, Geoffrey. "Angel." In *Evangelical Dictionary of Theology,* edited by Walter A. Elwell, 47-48. Grand Rapids: Baker Books, 1999.

Bruce, F. F. *Apostle of the Heart Set Free.* Grand Rapids, MI: Paternoster Press, 2000.

_____ *New Testament History.* New York, NY: Doubleday, 1980.

Caragounis, C. "Kingdom of God/Kingdom of Heaven." In *Dictionary of Jesus and the Gospels,* edited by Joel B. Green, 417-430. Downers Grove: InterVarsity Press, 1992.

Chavalas, M. "Moses." In *Dictionary of Old Testament Pentateuch,* edited by T. Desmond Alexander, 570-579. Downers Grove: InterVarsity Press, 2003.

Clouse, R. "Rapture of the Church." In *Evangelical Dictionary of Theology,* edited by Walter A. Elwell, 908-910. Grand Rapids: Baker Books, 1999.

Clowney, E. "Church." In *New Dictionary of Theology,* edited by Sinclair B. Ferguson, 140-143. Downers Grove: InterVarsity Press, 1988.

Colwell J. "Sin." In *New Dictionary of Theology,* edited by Sinclair Ferguson, 641-643. Downers Grove: InterVarsity Press, 1988.

Davidson, Maxwell. "Angels." In *Dictionary of Jesus and the Gospels,* edited by Joel B. Green, 8-11. Downers Grove: InterVarsity Press, 1992.

Dempster, Murray, Byron Klaus, and Douglas Peterson. *Called & Empowered: Global Mission in Pentecostal Perspective.* Peabody: Hendrickson Publishers, 2008.

Erickson, Millard *Christian Theology: Second Edition.* Grand Rapids, MI: Baker Academic, 2009.

Evans, Tony. *The Battle is the Lord's: Waging Victorious Spiritual Warfare,* Chicago, IL: Moody Publishers, 1998.

Frangipane, Francis. *The Three Battlegrounds: An In-depth View of Three Arenas in Spiritual Warfare: The Mind, the Church, and the Heavenly Places,* Cedar Rapids, IA: Arrow Publications, Inc., 2012.

Fretheim, G. "Exodus, Book of." In *Dictionary of Old Testament Pentateuch,* edited by T. Desmond Alexander, 249-258. Downers Grove: InterVarsity Press, 2003.

Gaffin Jr. R. "Kingdom of God." In *New Dictionary of Theology,* edited by Sinclair B. Ferguson, 367-369. Downers Grove: InterVarsity Press, 1988.

German, T. "Holy Spirit." In *Evangelical Dictionary of Theology,* edited Walter A. Elwell, 521-527. Grand Rapids: Baker Books, 1999.

GhanaWeb, "You Don't Have to Believe in God to Go to Heaven." file:///C:/Users/david/Downloads/You%20 don%E2%80%99t%20have%20to%20believe%20in%20 God%20to%20go%20to%20heaven%20_%20Religion%20 2013-09-12.htm (Accessed September 12, 2013).

BIBLIOGRAPHY

_____ Kenyan Cannibal Pleads Guilty to Killing, Eating Ghanaian Mate, http://www.ghheadlines.com/agency/daily-graphic/2013/534124/kenyan-cannibal-pleads-guilty-to-killing—eating-ghanaian-mate— — (Accessed on August 22, 2013)

Johnson, Ian B. "God is King: God's Sovereignty; His Eternal Kingdom." christian-oneness.org/about-God/chapter6.html. (Accessed June 2, 2013).

_____ "God is King: The Kingdom of God is Where God is King, not in world, but in power." christian-oneness.org/about-God/chapter6html. (Accessed June 2, 2013).

_____ "God is King: The Kingdom then Came to Earth in the Person of its King." christian-oneness.org/about-God/chapter-6html. (Accessed June 2, 2013).

_____ "God is King: God's Kingdom is Eternal and Unchanging, but Appears to us to Vary." christian-oneness.org/about-God/chapter6html. (Accessed June 2, 2013).

_____ "God is King: Adam's Sin Created Visible Division in the Kingdom." christian-oneness.org/about-God/chapter6html. (Accessed June 2, 2013).

_____ "God is King: The King Now Lives in Every Believer Through the Holy Spirit." christian-oneness.org /about-God/chapter6html. (Accessed June 2, 2013).

_____ "God is King: The Last Period is the Harvest, when Evil is Purged, and God's Absolute Invisible Kingdom Becomes Visible to All." (Accessed June 2, 2013).

Grant, Elizabeth. "Proclaiming Christ's Victory Over Unjust Social Structures & Practices."*Spiritual Warfare in Enrichment: Enriching and Equipping Spirit-filled Ministers, 18* no. 3 (June 2013): 60-66.

Gruenler, R. "Son of Man." In *Evangelical Dictionary of Theology,* edited by Walter A. Elwell. 1034-1036. Grand Rapids: Baker Books, 1999.

Guelich, Robert. "Mark, Gospel of." In *Dictionary of Jesus and the Gospel,* edited by Joel B. Green, 512-525. Downers Grove: InterVarsity Press, 1992.

Hollenweger, Walter *The Pentecostals*. Peabody, MA: Hendrickson Publishers, 1988.

Huff Post Politics, "Obama Pushes African Leaders on Gay Rights, Rebuked by Senegalese President, Macky Sall, http://www.huffingtonpost.com/2013/06/27 obama-africa-gay-rightsn-3512530html (Accessed September 2, 2013).

Hymns of Glorious Praise *Gospel. Publishing House* (Springfield, MO: 1969).

Kearsley, R. "Angels." In *New Dictionary of Theology,* edited by Sinclair B. Ferguson, 20-21. Downers Grove: InterVarsity, 1988.

Kosh, Kurt *The Devil's Alphabet,* Grand Rapids: MI, Kregel Publications, 1971.

Knauth, R. "Israelites." In *Dictionary of Old Testament Pentateuch,* edited by T. Desmond Alexander, 452-458. Downers Grove: InterVarsity Press, 2003.

Kruse, C. "Apostle." In *Dictionary of Jesus and the Gospel*, edited by Joel B. Green, 27-33. Downers Grove: InterVarsity Press, 1992.

Ladd, G. "Kingdom of Christ, God, Heaven." In *Evangelical Dictionary of Theology*, edited by Walter A. Elwell, 607-611. Grand Rapids: Baker Books, 1999.

LaSort, William, David Hubbard, and Fredric Bush. *Old Testament Survey*. Grand Rapids: William Eerdmans Publishing Company, 1996.

Liefeld, W. "Patriarch." In *Evangelical Dictionary of Theology*, edited by Walter A. Elwell. 829. Grand Rapids: Baker Books, 1999.

Louisiana Baptist University. "Statement of Faith." http://www.lbu.edu/statementoffaith.html (Accessed September 18, 2013).

Longacre, R. "Joseph." In *Dictionary of Old Testament Pentateuch*, edited by T. Desmond Alexander. 469-477. Downers Grove: InterVarsity Press, 2003.

Lowenberg, D. "Demonization and the Christian Life: How the Devil Influences Believers." *Spiritual Warfare in Enrichment: Enriching and Equipping Spirit-filled Ministers, 18,* no. 3 (June 2013): 86-97.

Love, Rick *Muslims, Magic and the Kingdom of God*. Pasadena, CA: William Carey Library, 2000.

Luter, A. and Sheri Klouda. "Isaac." In *Dictionary of Old Testament Pentateuch*, edited by T. Desmond Alexander. 445-450. Downers Grove: InterVarsity Press, 2003.

Macleod, D. "Sovereignty of God." In *New Dictionary of Theology,* edited Sinclair B. Ferguson. 654-656. Downers Grove: InterVarsity Press, 1988.

Malick, Faisal. *10 Amazing Muslims Touched by God.* Carol Stream, IL: Tyndale House Publishers, 2012.

Manso, Paul. *Attitude of Gratitude.* Accra, Ghana: Tent Media Publication, 2011.

Marshall, I. "Son of Man." In *Dictionary of Jesus and the Gospels,* edited by Joel B. Green. 775-781. Downers Grove: InterVarsity Press, 1992.

_____ "Church." In *Dictionary of Jesus and the Gospels,* edited by Joel B. Green. 122-125. Downers Grove: InterVarsity Press, 1992.

Martin, R. "Sonship." In *New Dictionary of Theology,* edited by Sinclair B. Ferguson. 651- 653. Downers Grove: InterVarsity Press, 1988.

Matthews, Warren. *World Religions.* Belmont, CA: Wadsworth, 2010.

McComiskey, T. "Angel of the Lord." In *Evangelical Dictionary of Theology,* edited by Walter A. Elwell. 47-48. Grand Rapids: Baker Books, 1999.

McDermott, Gerald. *God's Rivals: Why Has God Allowed Different Religions? Insights from the Bible and the Early Church.* Downers Grove, IL. IVP Academic, 2007.

McDowell, Josh, and Don Stewart. *Handbook of Today's Religions.* Nashville: Thomas Nelson Publishers, 1983.

McGee, J. Vernon. *David: A Man After God's Own Heart.* Nashville, TN: Thomas Nelson Publishers, 2000.

McGrath, Alister. *Christian Theology: An Introduction.* Cambridge, MA: Blackwell Publishers, 1994.

Merriam-Webster. *Merriam-Webster's Collegiate Dictionary.* Springfield, MA: Merriam-Webster Incorporated, 2005.

Modern Ghana. "President Mills, Prime Minister Cameron on Homosexual Rights."http://www.modernghana.com/news359362/1/president-mills-prime-mimnister-cameron-and-homosex.html (Accessed September 1, 2013).

_____"Pentecostal and Charismatic Churches call on President Mills." http://www.modernghana.com/news/371802/1/pentecostal-and-charismatic.group.callsonpreside.html (Accessed October 7, 2013).

Mounce. W. "Lake of Fire" in *Evangelical Dictionary of Theology* ed. Walter A. Elwell. 617-618. Grand Rapids: Baker Books, 1999.

Murphy, Ed. *A Handbook for Spiritual Warfare.* Nashville, TN: Thomas Nelson Inc., 2003.

National Organization for Women. "Del Martin and Phyllis Lyon Make History Again." http://www.now.org/issues/lgbi/021304lyon.marrtin.html (Accessed August 30, 2013).

Nigeria. "British PM Vows to Export Gay Marriage Nationwide." file:///C:/Users/david/Downloads/allAfrica.c%20Nigeria%20%20British%20PM%20Vows%20to%20Export%20Gay%20Marriage%20Worldwide%20%28Page%201%20of%202%29.htm (Accessed August 29, 2013).

Omanson, R. "The Church." In *Evangelical Dictionary of Theology,* edited by Walter A. Elwell. 231-233. Grand Rapids: Baker Books, 1999.

Osborne, W. "Babel." In *Dictionary of Old Testament Pentateuch* edited by T. Desmond Alexander. 73-75. Downers Grove: InterVarsity Press, 2003.

Packer, J. "God." In *New Dictionary of Theology,* edited by Sinclair B. Ferguson. 274-277.

Downers Grove: InterVarsity Press, 1988.

_____ "Holy Spirit." In *New Dictionary of Theology,* edited by Sinclair B. Ferguson. 316-319. Downers Grove: InterVarsity Press, 1988.

Pfeiffer, Eric. "Tammy Baldwin is Elected the First Openly Gay Senator."

http://news.yahoo.com/blogs/ticket/tammy-baldwin-elected-first-open-gay-senator-043558173—election .html (Accessed November 7, 2013).

Phillips, John. *Exploring the Gospel of John: An Expository Commentary.* Grand Rapids, MI: Kregel Publications, 2001.

_____ *Exploring Acts: An Expository Commentary.* Grand Rapids, MI: Kregel Publications, 2001.

Piggin, F. "Roman Catholicism." In *Evangelical Dictionary of Theology,* edited by Walter A. Elwell. 955-959. Grand Rapids: Baker Books, 1999.

BIBLIOGRAPHY

Reuters. "Al Qaeda Calls for Attacks Inside United States." file:///C:/Users/david/Downloads/Al%20Qaeda%20calls%20 for%20attacks%20inside%20United%20States%20-%20 Yahoo%20News.htm (Accessed September 12, 2013).

Ridderbos, H. "Kingdom of God, Kingdom of Heaven," edited by J. D. Douglas. 656-659.

Wheaton: Tyndale House Publishers Inc., 1982.

Rigsby, R. "Jacob." In *Dictionary of Old Testament Pentateuch*, edited by T. Desmond Alexander. 461-467. Downers Grove: InterVarsity Press, 2003.

Robinson, Phyllis. *Why I Believe the Bible is the Word of God.* Nashville, TN: Thomas Nelson Inc., 2012.

Saucy, R. "God, Doctrine of." In *Evangelic Dictionary of Theology,* edited by Walter A. Elwell. 459-464. Grand Rapids: Baker Books, 1999.

Spiritual Warfare. "Prepare Your Heart for Spiritual Warfare." www.battleinchrist.com (Accessed August, 17, 2013).

Stanton, G. "Praise." In *Evangelical Dictionary of Theology,* edited by Walter A. Elwell. 865-866. Grand Rapids: Baker Books, 1999.

Swindoll, Charles. *David: The Man of Passion and Destiny.* Nashville, TN: W. Publishing Group, 1997.

Tenney, M. "Pentecost." In *Evangelical Dictionary of Theology,* edited by Walter A. Elwell. 835. Grand Rapids: Baker Books, 1999.

The Huffington Post United Kingdom, "Australia's Prime Minister Kevin Rudd Pledges to Introduce Gay Marriage." file:///C:/Users/david/Downloads/Australia%27s%20Prime%20Minister%20Kevin%20Rudd%20Pledges%20To%20Introduce%20Gay%20Marriage.htm (Accessed September 2, 2013).

The Spiritual War: *What is Spiritual Warfare? Introduction to Spiritual Warfare—The Fall of Man.* http://www.truthnet.org/Spiritualwarfare/1SpiritualWarfare/Spiritual-warfare.htm (Accessed on August 17, 2013).

_____ *The Invisible World of the Spiritual Realms.* http://www.truthnet.org/Spiritualwarfare/1Spiritualwarfare/Spiritual-warfare.htm (Accessed on August 17, 2013).

_____ *When Did Spiritual Warfare Begin?* http://www.truthnet.org/Spiritual-warfare/1SpiritualWarfare/Spiritual-warfare.htm (Accessed on August 17, 2013).

Turner, M. "Holy Spirit." In *Dictionary of Jesus of Jesus and the Gospels,* edited by Joel B. Green. 341-351. Downers Grove: InterVarsity Press, 1992.

Twelftree, G. "Demon, Devil, Satan." In *Dictionary of Jesus and the Gospels,* edited by Joel B. Green. 163-172. Downers Grove: InterVarsity Press, 1992.

_____ "Temptations of Jesus." In *Dictionary of Jesus and the Gospels,* edited by Joel B. Green. 821-827. Downers Grove: InterVarsity Press, 1992.

_____ "Devil and Demons." In *New Dictionary of Theology* edited by Sinclair B. Ferguson. 196-198. Downers Grove: InterVarsity Press, 1988.

Unger, M. "Satan." In *Evangelical Dictionary of Theology,* edited by Walter A. Elwell. 972-973. Grand Rapids: Baker House, 1999.

Wade, John. *Acts: Unlocking the Scriptures for You.* Cincinnati, OH: Standard Publishing, 1991.

Walton, J. "Eden, Garden of." In *Dictionary of Old Testament Pentateuch,* edited by T. Desmond Alexander. 203-207. Downers Grove: InterVarsity Press, 2003.

_____ "Flood." In *Dictionary of Old Testament Pentateuch,* edited by T. Desmond Alexander. 315-326. Downers Grove: InterVarsity Press, 2003.

What is Spiritual Warfare: A Definition of Spiritual Warfare. http://www.battlefocused.org/article/what-is-spiritual-warfare/ (Accessed August 17, 2013).

_____ *Answers to some common allegations concerning the study of Spiritual Warfare-Dualism.* http://www.battlefocused.org/article/what-is-spiritual-warfare/ (Accessed August 17, 2013).

Williams, D. "Judas Iscariot." In *Dictionary of Jesus and the Gospels,* edited by Joel B. Green. 406-408. Downers Grove: InterVarsity Press, 1992.

Williams, Dave *The Miracle Result of Fasting: Your Secret Weapon In Spiritual Warfare,* Lansing, MI: Decapolis Publishing, 1997.

Williamson, P. "Abraham." In *Dictionary of Old Testament Pentateuch,* edited by T. Desmond Alexander. 8-17. Downers Grove: InterVarsity Press, 2003.

Witherington III, B. "John the Baptist." In *Dictionary of Jesus and the Gospels,* edited by Joel B. Green. 383-391. Downers Grove: InterVarsity Press, 1992.

Wood, George "The Armor of God: A Meditation on Ephesians 6: 10-20." *Spiritual Warfare in Enrichment: Enriching and Equipping Spirit-filled Ministers, 18* no 3 (June 2013): 48-52.

Woudstra, M. "Abraham." In *Evangelical Dictionary of Theology,* edited by Walter A. Elwell. 6-7. Grand Rapids: Baker House, 1999.

Wright, G. *Great People of the Bible and How they lived.* Pleasantville, NY: The Reader's Digest Association, Inc., 1979.